Greeks and Romans
Topics in Greek and Roman History

Greeks and Romans

Topics in Greek and Roman History

by

HUGH HOLLINGHURST, M.A.

Director of Studies, Crosby Chesterfield High School

Illustrated by

BRIAN ERSKINE, A.T.D.

Head of Art and Design, Crosby Chesterfield High School

HEINEMANN EDUCATIONAL BOOKS
LONDON

Heinemann Educational Books Ltd

LONDON EDINBURGH MELBOURNE AUCKLAND TORONTO
HONG KONG SINGAPORE KUALA LUMPUR
IBADAN NAIROBI JOHANNESBURG
NEW DELHI

ISBN 0 435 36406 5

© Hugh Hollinghurst 1974
First published 1974

Published by
Heinemann Educational Books Ltd
48 Charles Street, London W1X 8AH
Filmset in Photon Imprint 12 pt by
Richard Clay (The Chaucer Press), Ltd, Bungay, Suffolk
and printed in Great Britain by
Fletcher & Son, Ltd, Norwich

Contents

Contents

Contents

Acknowledgements

I should like to thank my former colleagues at Liverpool Collegiate School, Miss Y. Zeffert, Mr D. Manning-Fox and Mr A. Wilson for their advice and help with the revision of the work, and my wife for her encouragement, advice, help and understanding.

Acknowledgements are due to the following authors and publishers for permission to reprint copyright material:

Mary Renault and the Longman Group Ltd for extract from *The Lion in the Gateway*; Penguin Books Ltd for extract from *The Life of Alexander the Great*, translated by Aubrey de Selincourt (Penguin Classics, 1958) © the Estate of Aubrey de Selincourt, 1968; from Herodotus: *The Histories*, translated by Aubrey de Selincourt (Penguin Classics, 1954) © the Estate of Aubrey de Selincourt, 1954; from Livy: *The War with Hannibal* translated by Aubrey de Selincourt (Penguin Classics, 1965) © the Estate of Aubrey de Selincourt, 1965; from Plutarch: *Fall of the Roman Republic* translated by Rex Warner (Penguin Classics, 1958) © Rex Warner, 1958; from Thucydides: *The Peloponnesian War* translated by Rex Warner (Penguin Classics, 1954) © Rex Warner, 1954; from Aeschylus: *The Persians* in *Prometheus Bound and Other Plays* translated by Philip Vellacott (Penguin Classics, 1961) © Philip Vellacott, 1961; Rosemary Sutcliff and Hamish Hamilton Ltd for extract from *The Truce of the Games*; Carole Dale Snedeker and J. M. Dent & Sons Ltd for extract from *Theras, The Story of an Athenian Boy*; The Bodley Head for extracts from *Legions of the Eagle* by Henry Treece and *The Road to Sardis* by Stephanie Plowman; Geoffrey Trease and Macmillan for extract from *The Crown of Violet*; Naomi Mitchison and MacDonald for extract from *The Young Alexander the Great*; Pierre Grimal and Burke Publishing Co. Ltd for extract from *Stories of Alexander the Great*; Leonard

Acknowledgements

Cotterell and Evans Brothers Ltd for extracts from *The Great Invasion* and *Enemy of Rome*; Rosemary Sutcliff and Oxford University Press for extracts from *The Eagle of the Ninth*; Hans Baumann and Oxford University Press for extract from *I Marched with Hannibal*; Geoffrey Trease and Macmillan for extracts from *Word to Caesar*; Barbara Ker Wilson and Constable Young Books for extract from *Beloved of the Gods*.

The photographs are reproduced by permission of the following:
The Trustees of the British Museum: p. 23
The Mansell Collection: pp. 30, 45, 48, 85
Thames and Hudson: p. 53
Ente Provinciale per il Turismo, Cuneo: p. 65
Paul Elek Ltd: pp. 127, 131, 134
Alinari photography: p. 126

List of Illustrations and Maps

List of illustrations and maps

The cover picture shows Roman and Carthaginian boats grappling in the First Punic War (see p. 62).

At the start of the war the Romans were experienced soldiers and the Carthaginians expert sailors. The Romans invented a drawbridge that could be dropped on to the enemy's deck from their own. Their soldiers could then swarm across to capture the Carthaginian vessel. In this way they fought a land battle on the sea and made good use of their military experience.

The drawbridge was called a *corvus* ('raven') because of the large spike or beak on the end, which stuck in the enemy's deck. It can be seen in the raised position on the ship in the centre of the picture.

Introduction

Our civilization was born in Greece. The Ancient Greeks made the first discoveries in the skills and knowledge on which our civilization depends.

The Greeks were the first scientists. One of them nearly 2,500 years ago said that there were atoms and explained how they could form the universe. Even now when scientists make a new invention or discovery they use Greek words to form the new word, describing what they have found (for example: *telephone, hydro*-foil, *ballistic* missile).

The Greeks were great mathematicians and astronomers. One of them, two thousand years before Galileo, said that the sun was at the centre of the solar system and calculated the circumference of the earth (see the diagram on p. xiv).

The Greeks were the founders of our form of government—democracy, which is formed from two Greek words meaning 'power of the people'. (In what way is our country in the power of the people as a whole?)

The Greeks were the first historians and playwrights. Herodotus who wrote a history of the Persian Wars (see pp. 9–16) is called the 'Father of History'. Greek plays are frequently performed to this day and the myths acted out in them are still retold (see the first companion volume to this one, *Gods and Heroes of Ancient Greece*).

Many examples of their art and architecture survive and have been copied throughout the centuries. Most of our towns have examples of ancient Greek columns among their buildings. Look at some of the old important buildings in your town (for example the town hall) and see if you can find columns like those pictured on p. 31.

In the second century B.C. Greece was conquered by the Romans, who spread and preserved the learning of the Greeks because of their wide and long lasting empire. They also added their own contribution to the learning. To govern this empire,

Introduction

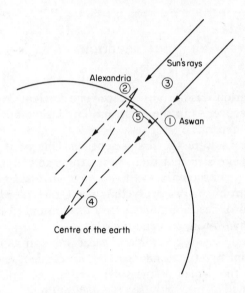

Centre of the earth

HOW ERATOSTHENES CALCULATED THE CIRCUMFERENCE OF THE EARTH

1. He discovered that the sun was vertical at Syene (Aswan) at noon on midsummer day.
2. He measured the angle of the shadow cast by a stick at Alexandria on the same day (one fiftieth of a circle).
3. The sun's rays coming as they do from such a great distance can be considered to be running parallel to each other when they reach the earth.
4. Therefore the angle at the centre of the earth is also one fiftieth of a circle (the two angles are 'alternate' and therefore equal).
5. The distance from Alexandria to Aswan is 5,000 stadia.*
6. Therefore the circumference of the earth is 50 times this, i.e. 250,000 stadia.
7. Eratosthenes altered this later to 252,000 stadia which is 24,662 miles, within 200 miles of the correct figure.

* A stadium is a Greek measure of length, about 200 yards.

which stretched 2,500 miles from east to west and half as much from north to south and which lasted for many centuries, they established an efficient civil service and a system of law which is still used in many countries to this day. Their engineering was superb; their roads were not to be surpassed until the eighteenth century, and many of their bridges and monuments stand today—and are still used. Latin, the language of the Romans, was spoken throughout their vast empire and from it come many modern European languages, called for this reason Romance languages. 60 per cent of our language is derived from Latin. In fact 60 per cent of this last sentence comes from Latin.

The periods of history and the events in this book show how these two civilizations grew, and depict what sort of life the Greeks and Romans led. Episodes illustrating memorable or everyday happenings have been chosen from historians or historical novels and these are linked by short passages of explanation so that the period of history can be read as a continuous story. At the end of each chapter activities of different kinds are suggested for you to do. By doing these you will get to know more about the beginnings of our own Western civilization and hence about the kind of life we now lead.

1 The Persian Wars

The civilization of the Greeks was nearly destroyed at its very beginning.

In 500 B.C. Greece was composed of small city states in constant rivalry and often at war with each other, as they were independent and valued their freedom more than anything else. The most important states were Athens and Sparta.

In 500 B.C. the Persian Empire was the biggest and most powerful that there had ever been in the Mediterranean area. The Persians had conquered the Babylonians in 538 B.C. (when Belshazzar saw the writing on the wall[1]) and their leader, Cyrus, started a line of kings which has lasted to this day—over 2,500 years. They soon went on to conquer the lands previously held by the Egyptians, Assyrians and many other middle and near eastern peoples until their empire stretched from India in the east to what is now Turkey in the west. This western part of their empire was composed of Greeks who had sent out colonies across the Aegean Sea to live in Ionia. In 499 B.C. these Ionian Greeks rebelled in an attempt to win freedom from the tyranny of Persia. They asked for help from the cities of Greece. Only Athens and Eretria sent help, just 25 ships altogether. After landing on the Ionian coast their crews marched inland and burnt the Persian capital of the province, Sardis. Although in the end the rebellion of the Ionian Greeks failed, the Persian King, Darius, was determined on revenge: he ordered one of his slaves to say three times whenever he had dinner 'Sire, remember the Athenians'.

In 490 B.C. Darius sent a huge army to Greece with orders to destroy Athens and Eretria. He could then go on to conquer the rest of Greece as well. The army sailed across the Aegean Sea, burnt Eretria and landed on the coast of Attica (the name of the country around Athens) at Marathon. When news of this was brought to Athens the Athenians had to decide what plan of war

[1] See the book of Daniel, chapter 5.

1

The Persian Wars

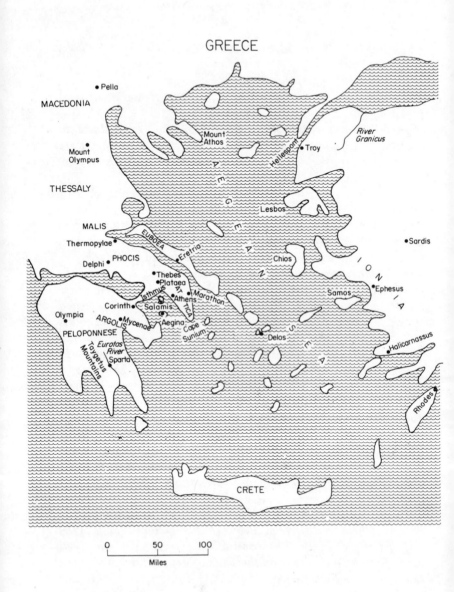

GREECE

Pella

MACEDONIA

Mount Olympus

THESSALY

Mount Athos

Hellespont

Troy

River Granicus

AEGEAN

Lesbos

MALIS

Thermopylae

EUBOEA

Delphi

PHOCIS

Eretria

Chios

Sardis

Thebes

Plataea

Marathon

Ionia

Isthmus

Corinth

Athens

ATTICA

Samos

Ephesus

Olympia

Salamis

ARGOLIS

Mycenae

Aegina

Cape Sunium

Delos

CYCLADES

Halicarnassus

PELOPONNESE

Eurotas River

Taygetus Mountains

Sparta

Rhodes

CRETE

0   50   100

Miles

2

*to adopt. Should they stay in the city or should they march out
to meet the Persians?*

The First 'Marathon'

So the leaders of Athens, the archons, met the generals in
council, and all agreed: 'If Eubœa[1] will not fight, we have only
one hope left. We must send word to Sparta.'

Now indeed it was time to remember the the fair-haired
Dorians[2] of the south.

Philosophers did not visit them, nor bards, nor carvers of
gems. They were ignorant, or forgetful, of all the arts save
one; but that they worked at from the cradle to the grave. The
art of Sparta was war.

The land they took in old days with their iron spears had
been famous for many centuries; Helen the Beautiful met
Paris there, and fled with him to Troy. But the Dorians were
harder and stronger, as iron is harder than bronze. They
burned the rich cities, killed the kings and warriors; but the
people they kept as slaves. Slaves were the wealth of the
ancient world; their labour set their masters free for hunting
and fighting and the pleasures of life. So the race of the Helots
still survived, but to a life of serfdom, tilling the fields of their
Spartan lords and herding their cattle.

There is an ancient proverb, '"Take what you want and pay
for it," says God.' The Spartans took, and paid. They were
tough and brave, but few. The Helots, though brought so low,
were many. As years and centuries passed, fear of a Helot
rising governed the Spartans' lives from birth till death.
Almost as soon as they could walk, they started to train for
battle, living rough and sleeping hard; never allowed to cry if
they were hungry, cold or in pain—which was often, for they
wore only one thin tunic summer or winter; were kept short
of food so that they would learn to live off the land; and, in
their boyhood, were taken to the temple once a year and
beaten till they bled, to try how well they bore it. Only strong

[1] Eubœa was the island on which Eretria stood.
[2] The Dorians and Ionians spoke different dialects of Greek.

3

boys survived to manhood; and if a baby looked sickly, they did not wait to see, but killed it when it was born. They had no time left for making music or the fine Laconian jars that once had been their pride; they ceased to question what men should be, or why, or how the world is made. They were at the other end of life from the Ionians.

Their boast was to be masters of the Helots, but to call no man master themselves. Though they still had kings, they had two at a time; descendants of twin brothers, it was said; and the power of the kings was strictly watched. In peace-time, they had to obey the Council of the Ephors; it was only when he led his troops to battle that a Spartan king's word was law. To the needs of war, everything else gave way. If a mother saw her son carried back dead on his shield by his comrades, she only asked if he had fallen bravely. If he had, it was thought a disgrace to weep.

So when the Athenians heard that the Persian host was near, they said, 'The Spartans will never endure a foreign yoke. If we send them word, they will march to help us.'

At first they meant to send a ship, which was the quickest way; but the winds were contrary; and a horse would have been useless, for no one yet had thought of shoeing horses, and it would have been lamed on the stony mountain roads. They said, 'We must send a runner.'

They went, therefore, to the chief gymnasium of Athens, where the athletes, stripped and rubbed down with oil, were at exercise, or training for the Games: wrestling, or throwing the javelin at the mark, or scuffling in the pancration, which was an all-in of wrestling and boxing mixed. The runners were practising the long jump, with stone weights in their hands to swing them farther—light lean young men, moving gracefully. The Greeks thought there was something wrong with any sport which did not make a man's whole body balanced and beautiful, as well as strong and quick. The Games were sacred to the gods, who asked perfection. While the young men jumped, a musician played on a flute, to give them rhythm.

The archons said to the trainer, 'Who is the best of all your runners?'

He answered at once, 'Pheidippides. At the All-Athenian Games in Athens he won the victor's wreath, and at the

4

Isthmian Games at Corinth; he was crowned too at Delphi, though men from the coast can seldom win in that mountain air. Now he is in training for Olympia itself, and I think he will bring back the olive garland, the crown of crowns.'

The archons said, 'May it be so; but that is for another day. You say he can run in the mountains? Good; bring him here.'

The trainer called. A young man left the line, and stood respectfully before them. Pheidippides, in Greek, means 'shining horse', and it suited him well. He was slim and limber, hard muscles moving sleekly under a skin polished like silk with the oil of the gymnasium. He looked swift, faithful and brave.

They told him his mission, and how much would hang on it. Then they gave him the written message, and taught him a speech as well, for there were many Spartans who could not read; when the war drills were finished, the boys were too tired to learn. He took a little bag of coins, which weighs lighter than food to carry, and a cloak of light wool for the cold nights in the mountains; and started on his way. Already, when he left, Eubœa had been taken. From the coasts of Attica they could look across the narrow strait at beaches black with Persian ships.

He did not see them; his road lay westward. First came the low green hills of Daphne,[1] with Apollo's laurel grove and shrine; then the road ran beside the water of the Straits of Salamis, through the plain of Eleusis. He saw, as he ran, the temple of Demeter the Mother, where he had been initiated into the Mysteries while he was still a boy. He remembered the wait in frightening darkness, then the great light, the singing, and the glorious sight that one must swear never to tell of, but which made one better for evermore. 'Holy Mother,' he prayed, 'Giver of perfect gifts, bless us now, and in our death-hour when we cross the River. I have drunk your mixed drink; I have carried my torch to the sea-shore . . .' Then he fell silent, lest even in solitude he might break his oath.

He passed the harbour, with the ships making for Salamis; but still the wind blew contrary, and he knew now he must run the whole of the way.

After he had passed through Megara, he came to the Isthmus, the narrow neck between the mainland and the Peloponnese. Here in old days the hero Theseus had cleared

[1] See the map on page 16 for the route from here to Megara.

5

the road from robbers and monsters who preyed upon its travellers, had wrestled with the murderer Sciron and thrown him off the cliff. The pale dusty track threaded the hillsides, and down below was the sea, deep blue and green, washing the feet of the dark crags. He longed to plunge down into it, to cool himself and sluice away the hot dust of the road. But he had measured his time, so much for food and rest, an hour or two for sleep, the least he could do with to keep going.

He sighted Corinth, the round-topped mountain wreathed with walls, and Isthmia where they held the Games of Poseidon, lord of the earthquake and the sea. There in the stadium he had waited at the starting stone, his toes against the grooves, while the umpire called out, 'Runners! Feet to the line!' He remembered the last lap, only the man from Sparta still in front; the gathering of his strength for the final sprint. But he was running now against unseen antagonists—time and fate.

Resting a little, and drinking from the streams, and eating sparely, he ran on and on, in high, hot noon and in the sunset and under the rising moon and in the grey of daybreak: up into the hills of Argolis, past the squat stone keep of Mycenæ, brooding on its ruined greatness and its ancient curse; then up and up, into the great range of Taygetus that bounds Sparta to the north. 'The hardest lap', he thought, 'will be coming last.'

He was up in the thin cold air, higher than the pure blue air of Delphi where he had been crowned in Apollo's temple on the mountainside. Here all was bare rock, and watercourses scoured as clean as bone; harsh thorn bushes and sparse scrub, a bare living for goats; around and above, more peaks, blue in the distance, veined in their cracks and gullies with frozen snow.

He had run at Delphi fresh; now he was weary; his chest was labouring, for every step he needed a new breath, the cold air seemed to stab his lungs like a sword. And he thought, 'I shall never run now at Olympia. This day has broken my strength; I feel a flaw in the iron, a crack in the jar, that won't be mended. They will never carve my name in marble, to be remembered for ever; never the wreath of wild olive, the crown of crowns ... But, if the Persians win, no more Olympia at all, no honour, no sacred games. Better than winning, to give them back to Hellas for evermore.'

He laboured on through the passes, skirting the edges of great black ravines, knowing one false step could send him down where only the wolves would find him; then out into the teeth of the wind. His heart was pounding when he stopped to rest, and he thought, 'I shall die if I go on. I cannot do it.' Then he thought of his city burned and sacked; his mother and little brothers carried away to slavery, and the girl he was in love with, dragged shrieking to the Persian ships. He had held nothing back; he was ready to die with that day's sunset if he could give his message first; but if he died here on the wild mountain, who would be the better for him but the vultures and the wolves? There was nothing to do but pray. He was far from the gods of home; but as he stumbled on, he panted out a prayer to whatever god might hear him.

When he opened his eyes, the dark mountains still swam around him. But his loneliness had left him, and the fear of the empty places; it seemed to him now that the wilderness had become his friend, and he was alone no longer.

Someone was keeping pace with him, breathing like a runner with strength to spare; he heard the steady rhythm, yet there was no thud of feet, only the click of trotting hoofs. His sight was dimmed with blackouts coming and going; but when it cleared he saw beside him horns, a long goat beard, and strange yellow eyes. And he thought, in the dream of his great weariness, 'It is Pan, driver of herds, lord of the wastelands; the god of the place, to whom I prayed.'

He uttered in his dream some salutation; his lips did not move, he was running with all his breath; and it seemed that Pan replied to him, mixed with a wild music like a reed pipe in the wind, 'You all forgot me in the city; yet I am here.' The echoes came back from the iron rocks and gullies. 'I am here ... I am here ...!'

The shaggy god was close to him, he caught the rank, strong goat smell, and heard the kicked pebbles fly. 'I am your friend, Pheidippides, Shining Horse of Athens. I was honoured once in Attica, before men lived in cities. Why do they forget?'

So he ran in a kindly dream, with Pan beside him, who could stampede great herds of cattle with a breaking twig, or send a man in headlong flight, without reason, through a lonely wood, so that he would say later, 'Why did I run? It was panic, the madness of the god.' But he felt no fear, only a comfort, as if some great friendly beast had come to keep him company. At last he came into the foothills, where the going was downhill and the air was stronger. His head and his eyes grew clear, and he found himself alone. No living creature was in sight, save a wild he-goat standing on a crag; but he knew he could get to Sparta now, before his strength gave out.

At last he came to the city of thatched huts beside the broad stream of Eurotas (the Spartans had no time to spare for carving marble) and the people crowded round him to hear the news. When they learned that in two days he had run a hundred and fifty miles, they said, 'Not bad.' It was a point of pride with the Spartans to waste no words.

After he had rested for a while, and drunk some wine, he came before the Council of the Ephors. When they had heard his message, they all agreed that the Persians must not rule in Hellas; that troops should be sent to Attica to man the coast. 'But,' they said, 'it is the moon's first half, and we start no new business before full moon. That is our ancient law.'

'But,' said Pheidippides, who could scarcely believe his ears, 'that is not for five days! Marching with heavy arms, it will take you five more to get there. And the Persians, if they cross the straits to Marathon, can be at Athens in a day.'

'That is with the gods,' said the eldest ephor. 'Here in Sparta, the customs are never changed.'

Pheidippides went to his bed of rushes in the guest hut, heavy of heart. Though the bed was rough, he was tired enough to have slept on marble. He thought, before he closed his eyes, 'In Athens, when we were ruled by Hippias, we called it tyranny. It seems there is another kind that men make in their own souls. As boys they must question nothing; as youths they must think alike, what they are told. And when they are men, there is a fetter of iron around their minds.'

Next day he went down to the coast, for the wind that had stopped his sailing there would blow him home. He thought of Pan, and the struggle that had almost killed him, and how he would never run, now, at Olympia with his strained heart. It would have been all the same, he thought, if he had taken it easy, bathing in the cool rock pools, resting in the heat of noon, saving his strength for Olympia and the glorious olive crown. And indeed his name was never carved in marble and put up in the temple of Olympian Zeus. But the temple has fallen, the carved names have been gone a thousand years; while famous Herodotus, who wrote the history of the war, put in the story of his run, and how he met Pan in the mountains. Because of him and the battle he brought warning of, a long cross-country run is still called a Marathon; and his name has come down with honour to our own day.

The Spartans did send help in the end, but it was too late: the battle had already taken place. The Athenians had marched out to the plain of Marathon with their whole army of 10,000 men, helped by the Plataeans, the only Greeks to send help in time, with their whole army of 1,000 men. The Persian force outnumbered them many times over. Herodotus, a Greek historian called the Father of History, wrote a history of the Persian Wars from which the following description of the battle is taken.

The Battle of Marathon

One result of the disposition of Athenian troops before the battle was the weakening of their centre by the effort to extend the line sufficiently to cover the whole Persian front; the two wings were strong, but the line in the centre was only a few ranks deep. The dispositions made, and the preliminary sacrifice promising success, the word was given to move, and

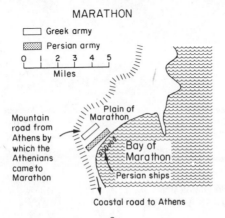

MARATHON

GREEK HOPLITE AND PERSIAN

The Greek hoplite ('heavy armed soldier') was equipped with a spear for stabbing the enemy. He fought in a mass of soldiers in close, ordered ranks called a phalanx. The shield was usually decorated, often with a badge of the soldier's own city. The sword was for use in emergency if the spear was broken or lost.

The Persian armour varied depending upon which country of the Persian Empire the soldier came from. The Persian equipment and armour was much lighter than that of the Greeks and the dress was decorated in bright colours. See the history of Herodotus, book 7, chapters 61 to 80, for the different types of armour.

the Athenians advanced at a run towards the enemy, not less than a mile away. The Persians, seeing the attack developing at the double, prepared to meet it confidently enough, for it seemed to them suicidal madness for the Athenians to risk an assault with so small a force—at the double, too, and with no support from either cavalry or archers. Well, that was what they imagined; nevertheless, the Athenians came on, closed with the enemy all along the line, and fought in a way not to be forgotten. They were the first Greeks, so far as I know, to charge at a run, and the first who dared to look without flinching at Persian dress and the men who wore it; for until that day came, no Greek could hear even the word Persian without terror.

The struggle at Marathon was long drawn out. In the centre, held by the Persians themselves and the Sacae, the advantage was with the foreigners, who were so far successful as to break the Greek line and pursue the fugitives inland from the sea; but the Athenians on one wing and the Plataeans on the other were both victorious. Having got the upper hand, they left the defeated Persians to make their escape, and then, drawing the two wings together into a single unit, they turned their attention to the Persians who had broken through in the centre. Here again they were triumphant, chasing the routed enemy, and cutting them down as they ran right to the edge of the sea.

The Persians lost 6,400 men, the Athenians 192.

After this, the Persians were even more determined on revenge. Darius died and the new king Xerxes made massive preparations. He collected from all parts of his empire a force of a quarter of a million, which seemed to the Greek historian Herodotus like five million and capable of drinking rivers dry. He then advanced to the Hellespont where he had a bridge of boats built to transport the army across. The bridge was destroyed by a storm, but Xerxes had the Hellespont whipped soundly for its behaviour and ordered the engineers' heads to be cut off. More engineers then built a new bridge and the army crossed safely. The army and navy kept pace with each other as they followed the northern coast of the Aegean Sea and advanced into Greece from the north. The Greeks, who had had ample time to make preparations themselves, held a council of war and sent a force northwards to try to stem the Persians' advance. So when the Persians reached Thermopylae where the mountains come down close to the sea, they found the way blocked by a small Greek force led by Leonidas and 300 Spartans. This description also comes from the Greek historian Herodotus.

The Battle of Thermopylae

For four days Xerxes waited, in constant expectation that the Greeks would make good their escape; then, on the fifth, when still they had made no move and their continued presence seemed mere impudent and reckless folly, he was seized with rage and sent forward the Medes and Cissians with orders to take them alive and bring them into his presence. The Medes charged, and in the struggle which ensued many fell; but others took their places, and in spite of terrible losses refused

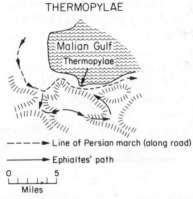

THERMOPYLAE

- - - -▶ Line of Persian march (along road)

──────▶ Ephialtes' path

0 ... 5 Miles

to be beaten off. They made it plain enough to anyone, and not least to the king himself, that he had in his army many men, indeed, but few soldiers. All day the battle continued; the Medes, after their rough handling, were at length withdrawn and their place was taken by Hydarnes and his picked Persian troops—the King's Immortals—who advanced to the attack in full confidence of bringing the business to a quick and easy end. But, once engaged, they were no more successful than the Medes had been; all went as before, the two armies fighting in a confined space, the Persians using shorter spears than the Greeks and having no advantage from their numbers.

On the Spartan side it was a memorable fight; they were

men who understood war pitted against an inexperienced
enemy, and amongst the feints they employed was to turn
their backs in a body and pretend to be retreating in confusion, whereupon the enemy would come on with a great
clatter and roar, supposing the battle won; but the Spartans,
just as the Persians were on them, would wheel and face them
and inflict in the new struggle innumerable casualties. The
Spartans had their losses too, but not many. At last the
Persians, finding that their assaults upon the pass, whether by
divisions or by any other way they could think of, were all
useless, broke off the engagement and withdrew. Xerxes was
watching the battle from where he sat; and it is said that in the
course of the attacks three times, in terror for his army, he
leapt to his feet.

Next day the fighting began again, but with no better
success for the Persians, who renewed their onslaught in the
hope that the Greeks, being so few in number, might be badly
enough disabled by wounds to prevent further resistance. But
the Greeks never slackened; their troops were ordered in
divisions corresponding to the states from which they came,
and each division took its turn in the line except the Phocian,
which had been posted to guard the track over the mountains.
So when the Persians found that things were no better for
them than on the previous day, they once more withdrew.

How to deal with the situation Xerxes had no idea; but
while he was still wondering what his next move should be, a
man from Malis got himself admitted to his presence. This
was Ephialtes, the son of Eurydemus, and he had come, in
hope of a rich reward, to tell the king about the track which
led over the hills to Thermopylae—and the information he
gave was to prove the death of the Greeks who held the pass.

Xerxes found Ephialtes' offer most satisfactory. He was
delighted with it, and promptly gave orders to Hydarnes to
carry out the movement with the troops under his command.
They left camp about the time the lamps are lit.

By early dawn they were at the summit of the ridge, near
the spot where the Phocians, as I mentioned before, stood on
guard with a thousand men, to watch the track and protect
their country. The Phocians were ready enough to undertake
this service, and had, indeed, volunteered for it to Leonidas,

knowing that the pass at Thermopylae was held as I have already described.

The ascent of the Persians had been concealed by the oak-woods which cover this part of the mountain range, and it was only when they reached the top that the Phocians became aware of their approach; for there was not a breath of wind, and the marching feet made a loud swishing and rustling in the fallen leaves. Leaping to their feet, the Phocians were in the act of arming themselves when the enemy was upon them. The Persians were surprised at the sight of troops preparing to resist; they had not expected any opposition—yet here was a body of men barring their way. Hydarnes asked Ephialtes who they were, for his first uncomfortable thought was that they might be Spartans; but on learning the truth he prepared to engage them. The Persian arrows flew thick and fast, and the Phocians, supposing themselves to be the main object of the attack, hurriedly withdrew to the highest point of the mountain, where they made ready to face destruction. The Persians, however, with Ephialtes and Hydarnes paid no further attention to them, but passed on along the descending track with all possible speed.

The Greeks at Thermopylae had their first warning of the death that was coming with the dawn from the seer Megistias, who read their doom in the victims of sacrifice; deserters, too, had begun to come in during the night with news of the Persian movement to take them in the rear, and, just as day was breaking, the look-out men had come running from the hills. At once a conference was held, and opinions were divided, some urging that they must on no account abandon their post, others taking the opposite view. The result was that the army split: some dispersed, the men returning to their various homes, and others made ready to stand by Leonidas.

In the morning Xerxes poured a libation to the rising sun, and then waited till about the time of the filling of the market-place, when he began to move forward. This was according to Ephialtes' instructions, for the way down from the ridge is much shorter and more direct than the long and circuitous ascent. As the Persian army advanced to the assault, the Greeks under Leonidas, knowing that the fight would be their last, pressed forward into the wider part of the pass much

14

further than they had done before; in the previous days' fighting they had been holding the wall and making sorties from
behind it into the narrow neck, but now they left the confined
space and battle was joined on more open ground. Many of the
invaders fell; behind them the company commanders plied
their whips, driving the men remorselessly on. Many fell into
the sea and were drowned, and still more were trampled to
death by their friends. No one could count the number of the
dead. The Greeks, who knew that the enemy were on their way
round by the mountain track and that death was inevitable,
fought with reckless desperation, exerting every ounce of
strength that was in them against the invader. By this time
most of their spears were broken, and they were killing
Persians with their swords.

In the course of that fight Leonidas fell, having fought like a
man indeed. Many distinguished Spartans were killed at his
side—their names, like the names of all the three hundred, I
have made myself acquainted with, because they deserve to be
remembered. Amongst the Persian dead, too, were many men
of high distinction—for instance, two brothers of Xerxes,
Habrocomes and Hyperanthes, both of them sons of Darius by
Artanes' daughter Phratagune.

There was a bitter struggle over the body of Leonidas; four
times the Greeks drove the enemy off, and at last by their
valour succeeded in dragging it away. So it went on, until the
fresh troops with Ephialtes were close at hand; and then, when
the Greeks knew that they had come, the character of the
fighting changed. They withdrew again into the narrow neck
of the pass, behind the walls, and took up a position in a single
compact body—all except the Thebans—on the little hill at
the entrance to the pass, where the stone lion in memory of
Leonidas stands to-day. Here they resisted to the last, with
their swords, if they had them, and, if not, with their hands
and teeth, until the Persians, coming on from the front over
the ruins of the wall and closing in from behind, finally overwhelmed them.

*The Persians marched on and burnt Athens. The Athenians
had escaped to the neighbouring island of Salamis and the
Greek fleet was stationed in between the island and the main-*

land. *The Spartans wanted to abandon Athens and retreat to the Isthmus of Corinth; the Athenians wanted to stay close to Athens and fight. This the Athenian commander Themistocles ensured by a trick. He sent a message to Xerxes, pretending to be a traitor, saying that the Greeks intended to retreat: if he sent part of his fleet round the island to the rear of the Greeks to prevent their retreat and attacked immediately he would win. Xerxes followed this advice and the Greeks, finding that they could not retreat, were forced to fight—as Themistocles and the Athenians wanted.*

Aeschylus, an Athenian who saw the battle, later wrote a play called The Persians. *One of the characters in the play is a Persian messenger who gives news of the battle to the Queen in Persia.*

The Battle of Salamis

A Hellene[1] from the Athenian army came and told
Your son Xerxes this tale: that, once the shades of night
Set in, the Hellenes would not stay, but leap on board,
And, by whatever secret route offered escape,
Row for their lives. When Xerxes heard this, with no
  thought

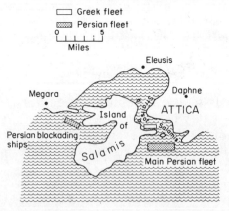

SALAMIS

---

[1] The Greeks called themselves Hellenes and their country Hellas (as on their stamps today).

The Battle of Salamis

Of the man's guile, or of the jealousy of gods,
He sent this word to all his captains: 'When the sun
No longer flames to warm the earth, and darkness holds
The court of heaven, range the main body of our fleet
Threefold, to guard the outlets and the choppy straits.'
Then he sent other ships to row right round the isle,
Threatening that if the Hellene ships found a way through
To save themselves from death, he would cut off the head
Of every Persian captain. By these words he showed
How ignorance of the gods' intent had dazed his mind.

Our crews, then, in good order and obediently,
Were getting supper; then each oarsman looped his oar
To the smooth rowing-pin; and when the sun went down
And night came on, the rowers all embarked, and all
The heavy-armed soldiers; and from line to line they called,
Cheering each other on, rowing and keeping course
As they were ordered. All night long the captains kept
Their whole force cruising to and fro across the strait.
Now night was fading; still the Hellenes showed no sign
Of trying to sail out unnoticed; till at last
Over the earth shone the white horses of the day,
Filling the air with beauty. Then from the Hellene ships
Rose like a song of joy the piercing battle-cry,
And from the island crags echoed an answering shout.

The Persians knew their error; fear gripped every man.
They were no fugitives who sang that terrifying
Paean,[1] but Hellenes charging with courageous hearts
To battle. The loud trumpet flamed along their ranks.
At once their frothy oars moved with a single pulse,
Beating the salt waves to the bo'suns' chant; and soon
Their whole fleet hove clear into view; their right wing first,
In precise order, next their whole array came on,
And at that instant a great shout beat on our ears:
'Forward, you sons of Hellas! Set your country free!
Set free your sons, your wives, tombs of your ancestors,
And temples of your gods. All is at stake: now fight!'
Then from our side in answer rose the manifold
Clamour of Persian voices; and the hour had come.

[1] The battle song of the Greeks.

The Persian Wars

GREEK TRIREME

The Greek *tri*reme was a warship with *three* banks of oars. In battle, only the oars were used and the sail was furled. The tactics were to sink your opponent's vessel by ramming it or to disable it by smashing the oars. Marines were usually carried who would fire javelins at the enemy or board their ships in close fighting and capture them.

At once ship into ship battered its brazen beak.
A Hellene ship charged first, and chopped off the whole stern
Of a Phoenician galley. Then charge followed charge
On every side. At first by its huge impetus
Our fleet withstood them. But soon, in that narrow space,
Our ships were jammed in hundreds; none could help
    another.
They rammed each other with their prows of bronze; and
    some
Were stripped of every oar. Meanwhile the enemy
Came round us in a ring and charged. Our vessels heeled
Over; the sea was hidden, carpeted with wrecks
And dead men; all the shores and reefs were full of dead.

Then every ship we had broke rank and rowed for life.
The Hellenes seized fragments of wrecks and broken oars

And hacked and stabbed at our men swimming in the sea
As fishermen kill tunnies or some netted haul.
The whole sea was one din of shrieks and dying groans,
Till night and darkness hid the scene. If I should speak
For ten days and ten nights, I could not tell you all
That day's agony. But know this: never before
In one day died so vast a company of men.

Xerxes, afraid that he might be trapped in Greece, fled with part of his army and the remainder of his fleet back to Persia. But most of the army he left behind with his son-in-law, Mardonius, who stayed in central Greece. Next year the Greeks marched out in full force and, largely due to the superb fighting qualities of the Spartans, defeated the Persians at Plataea. The threat of Persian tyranny over Greece had ended. Greece was safe, free to develop the ideas and knowledge which would benefit future civilizations.

Suggested Activities

Writing

1. Imagine you were Pheidippides. Describe your run from Athens to Sparta. (What sort of country did you go through? What were the names of the towns? How did you feel at each stage? What kept you going?)

2. Make a list of the battles of the Persian Wars and put by the side in columns the date of each battle, whether it was on land or sea and who won it. You could extend the list to include the names of the commanders and something special about each battle.

3. Imagine that you were a Greek or Persian fighting in one of the battles of the Persian Wars. Describe what happened in the battle.

4. Produce a newspaper for the Greeks or Persians after one of the battles. Include special reports from war correspondents, interviews, obituaries, pictures, maps, etc. A group of you could join together for this activity and each contribute something which could be pasted on to a large sheet of paper.

19

The Persian Wars

Drawing

1. Make a drawing of the god Pan as Pheidippides saw him.

2. Draw a map of Greece and the Persian Empire showing the difference in size between the two by colouring them. You could mark in some famous events connected with the wars, e.g. the run of Pheidippides, the routes of the Persian expeditions and the sites of the battles (see pp. 2 and 44).

3. Draw maps of the battles using different colours to show the land, the sea, the mountains and the Greek and Persian armies (see pp. 9, 12 and 16).

4. Draw a picture of a Greek and Persian soldier (see p. 10). You could draw them fighting each other, or a group fighting.

5. Draw a picture of a Greek trireme (see p. 18) or Greek and Persian triremes in action.

Acting

Write and act your own play called *The Persians*. The scene of the original play by Aeschylus is set in the Persian capital just before the news arrives of the battle of Salamis. A group (called a chorus) of Persian elders say how anxious they are for the army, and Atossa, mother of Xerxes, the Persian King, tells of a frightening dream she has had. A messenger arrives and describes the defeat of the Persians at Salamis (see pp. 16–19). The chorus call up the ghost of the previous Persian King, Darius, who says that the Persians lost because of the gods' anger at Xerxes' pride in having the Hellespont whipped. He foretells the future defeat of the Persians at Plataea. Xerxes arrives but, although the Persians are glad that he has come home safely, they are saddened by the defeat at Salamis and the thought of more disaster to come at Plataea.

Finding Out

1. Find out how Greek civilization developed before the Persian Wars (see the books listed under *Further Reading*, section 2).

2. Find out more about the Persians and the empires that the Persians took over before they attacked Greece (see

Suggested Activities

Assyrians, Babylonians, Egyptians, Lydians and Phoenicians among others).

3. You will find a more complete list of the peoples of the Persian Empire in Herodotus' *Histories*, book 7, chapters 61–95. List and illustrate the weapons and armour described by Herodotus.

4. Thermopylae means 'warm gates' because there were some warm springs of water by the pass which was like a gateway to central Greece. Thermos in Greek means 'warm'. What other words in English have thermo- in them and are connected with warmth? What other words in English come from Greek?

5. Find out what ships were like before the Greeks and how they have developed up until the present day.

Further Reading

ON THE PERSIAN WARS

Herodotus, *Histories*, translated by Aubrey de Selincourt, Penguin Classics.
Mary Renault, *The Lion in the Gateway*.
B. W. J. G. Wilson and D. J. D. Miller, *Stories from Herodotus*.

ON GREECE BEFORE THE PERSIAN WARS

J. Bolton, *Ancient Crete and Mycenae*, Then and There series.
H. E. L. Mellersh, *Finding Out about the Trojans*.
E. Royston Pike, *Finding Out about the Minoans*.
Frances Wilkens, *Ancient Crete*, Young Historian series.

2 Athens: Golden Age and Defeat

The Persians had been driven out of Greece but still ruled the Greeks in Ionia, and the Ionians had to be freed. Sparta, unadventurous, with only a land army, did nothing; Athens, adventurous and ambitious, with a large fleet, freed the Greek cities of Ionia. She then formed these cities and all the islands in the Aegean Sea into an alliance strong enough to withstand any threat from the Persians. Thus her empire started and during the following fifty years Athens grew in power and prosperity while Sparta and her allies grew more jealous and fearful. The two states became hostile towards one another and for a short time they were at war. Every four years, however, all Greek cities made a truce so that they could take part in the Olympic Games. Athenians and Spartans would join in friendly competition as this description of the foot-race shows: Amyntas was an Athenian and Leon a Spartan who had met for the first time at the Games and become great friends.

The Race at Olympia

'Now it's us!' someone said; and the boys were sprinting down the covered way, out into the open sun-drenched space of the Stadium.

The turf banks on either side of the broad track, and the lower slopes of the Kronon Hill that looked down upon it were packed with a vast multitude of onlookers. Half-way down on the right-hand side, raised above the tawny grass on which everybody else sat, were the benches for the Council, looking across to the white marble seat opposite, where the Priestess of Demeter, the only woman allowed at the Games, sat as still as though she herself were carved from marble, among all the jostling, swaying, noisy throng. Men were raking over the silver sand on the track. The trumpeter stood ready.

22

PERICLES

They had taken their places now behind the long white limestone curbs of the starting line. The Umpire was calling: 'Runners! Feet to the lines!'

Amyntas felt the scorching heat of the limestone as he braced the ball of his right foot into the shaped groove. All the

23

Athens: Golden Age and Defeat

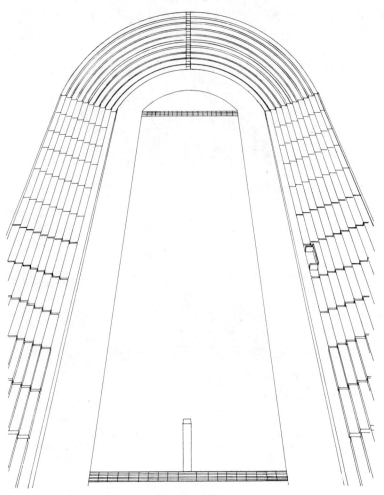

GREEK STADIUM

The Greeks held their athletics meetings in a 'stadium', so called because the length of the running track was 200 yards, a unit which the Greeks called a Stadium. All races finished at the rounded end where the largest number of spectators could get the best view. There were four different races:

1. One length, starting at the near end in the picture to finish at the far end.
2. Two lengths starting at the far end with the runners going round the turning post and finishing at the far end.
3. A long distance race with the runners going many times round turning posts placed at either end.

panic of a while back had left him, he felt light, and clear headed, and master of himself. He had drawn the sixth place, with Leon on his left and the boy from Megara on his right. Before him the track stretched white in the sunlight, an infinity of emptiness and distance.

The starting trumpet yelped; and the line of runners sprang forward like a wave of hunting dogs slipped from the leash.

Amyntas was running smoothly and without hurry. Let the green front-runners push on ahead. In this heat they would have burned themselves out before they reached the turning post. He and Leon were running neck and neck with the red-headed Macedonian. The Rhodian had gone ahead now after the front runners, the rest were still bunched. Then the Corinthian made a sprint and passed the boy from Rhodes, but fell back almost at once. The white track was reeling back underfoot, the turning post racing towards them. The bunch had thinned out, the front-runners beginning to drop back already; and as they came up towards the turning post, first the boy from Macedon, and then Nikomedes catching fire at last, slid into the lead, with Amyntas and Leon close behind them. Rounding the post, Amyntas skidded on the loose sand and Leon went ahead; and it was then, seeing the lean scarred back ahead of him, that Amyntas lengthened his stride, knowing that the time had come to run. They were a quarter of the way down the home lap when they passed Nikomedes; the Megaran boy had taken fire too late. They were beginning to overhaul the redhead; and Amyntas knew in his bursting heart that unless something unexpected happened, the race must be between himself and Leon. Spartan and Macedonian were going neck and neck now; the position held for a few paces, and then the redhead gradually fell behind. Amyntas was going all out, there was pain in his breast and belly and in the backs of his legs, and he did not know where his next breath was coming from; but still the thin scarred back was just ahead.

---

4. A two length race in armour.
There were permanent stone starting blocks at each end of the stadium. The runners placed their feet in the grooves when starting the race. The judges' seats can be seen half way along the stadium on the right.

The other events were the long jump, throwing the discus and javelin, wrestling, boxing and all-in wrestling.

The crowd were beginning to give tongue, seeing the two come through to the front; a solid roar of sound that would go on rising now until they passed the finishing post. And then suddenly Amyntas knew that something was wrong; Leon was labouring a little, beginning to lose the first keen edge of his speed. Snatching a glance downwards, he saw a fleck of crimson in the sand. The cut had re-opened.

His body went on running, but for a sort of splinter of time his head seemed quite apart from the rest of him, and filled with an unmanageable swirl of thoughts and feelings. Leon might have passed the top of his speed anyway, it might be nothing to do with his foot—but the cut *had* re-opened. . . . To lose the race because of a cut foot. . . . It would be so easy not to make that final desperate effort that his whole body was crying out against. Then Leon would keep his lead. . . . And at the same time another part of himself was remembering his father standing on the quayside at Piraeus as the *Paralos* drew away—crying out that he was not running only for himself but for Athens, his City and his people. . . . A crown of wild olive would be the greatest thing that anyone could give to his friend. . . . It would be to insult Leon to let him win . . . you could not do that to your friend. . . . And then like a clean cold sword of light cutting through the swirling tangle of his thoughts, came the knowledge that greater than any of these things were the Gods. These were the Sacred Games, not some mere struggle between boys in the gymnasium. For one fleeting instant of time he remembered himself standing in the Temple before the great statue of Zeus, holding the tiny bronze bull with the silvered horns. 'Let me run the best race that is in me, and think of nothing more.'

He drove himself forward in one last agonizing burst of speed, he was breathing against knives, and the roar of the blood in his ears drowned the roar of the crowd. He was level with Leon—and then there was nothing ahead of him but the winning post.

The onlookers had crowded right down towards it; even above the howl of the blood in his head he heard them now, roar on solid roar of sound, shouting him in to victory. And then Hippias had caught him as he plunged past the post; and he was bending over the trainer's arm, bending over the pain

26

in his belly, snatching at his breath and trying not to be sick. People were throwing sprigs of myrtle, he felt them flicking and falling on his head and shoulders. The sickness eased a little and his head was clearing; he began to hear friendly voices congratulating him; and Eudorus came shouldering through the crowd with a coloured ribbon to tie round his head. But when he looked round for Leon, the Spartan boy had been swept away by his trainer. And a queer desolation rose in Amyntas and robbed his moment of its glory.

So great and so many were the Athenian achievements at this time under her leader Pericles that it has been called the Golden Age of Athens.

Athens extended her naval empire to include all the islands in the Aegean Sea and most of the cities around it. She became a centre of learning for a thousand years, first among the Greeks and then among the Romans as well when they took over Greece. In Athens great thinkers continually sought for reasons for the behaviour and existence of the universe and mankind. Their discoveries paved the way for modern scientific progress. Each year the Athenians held festivals of plays which attracted visitors from all parts of Greece, and these plays are still performed regularly to this day. Athenian artists created work of outstanding beauty. An Athenian sculptor, Pheidias, made one of the seven wonders of the ancient world, a statue of Zeus in gold and ivory which stood in his temple at Olympia. Pheidias also contributed towards one of Athens' greatest achievements, the building of the temple called the Parthenon (which means 'temple of the maiden goddess')· dedicated to Athene (Athena), the patron goddess of Athens. In the following story Theras, an Athenian boy, goes with his father, Pheidon, to visit the temple.

The Parthenon

Right before them stood the goddess Athena herself, giant high, made of bright bronze, five times taller than a mortal man. She wore a helmet on her head, and carried aloft a spear. The sunlight touched the helmet so that it shone like a mirror, and the tip of the spear seemed to be afire.

27

Athens: Golden Age and Defeat

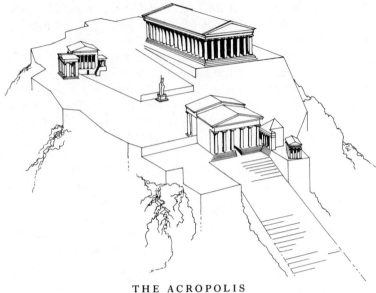

THE ACROPOLIS

The Acropolis ('Upper City') was the hill on which the Athenians first built their fortifications and later some of their magnificent temples.

The Panathenaic procession (see page 40) approached the Acropolis by the steps in the foreground of the picture. It went through the Propylaea ('Fore Gates') at the top of the steps, passed the statue of Athene and went up the ramp to the temple called the Parthenon ('Temple of the Maiden Goddess'). This was dedicated to Athene, the patron goddess of Athens, and the robe carried in the procession was placed on the knees of the gold and ivory statue of Athene in her temple.

The little temple of Wingless Victory, on the right of the Propylaea, was dedicated by the Athenians during the Peloponnesian War in the hope that victory might never fly away from Athens.

The temple called the Erechtheum, on the left of the Parthenon, was dedicated to Erechtheus, one of the early kings of Athens.

'Athena, Athena!' cried Theras, stretching up his hands in prayer to her. 'My dear goddess.'

Shivers of delight ran up and down his back. Pheidon knew that it was only a *statue* of Athena, but to Theras it seemed the goddess herself.

I do not blame him, for so beautiful was this Athena that I would willingly go twice around the world to see her.

The most important person in Athens—by far the most important—was Athena.

She was more important than Pheidon who was a judge,

28

than Euripides who was a great poet, than Pericles who was the most prominent citizen of the city.

'But,' you will object, 'Athena was not a *person*. She was only a goddess, a sort of myth. How could she be important?'

She was important because all the people in Athens except a few philosophers believed in her.

To the Athenians she stood in the place of God Himself.

The Athenians thought there were many gods: Zeus, who made the thunder and who owned all the bright sky; Hermes, who had wings on his heels and took you on your journeys; Artemis, the goddess of little girls. Little girls must always give their toys to Artemis when they grew up. There were many gods and goddesses—so the Greeks thought—and each city had a god or goddess all its own.

Athena was the goddess of Athens. She loved Athens more than any other city. Some people even thought she lived in a house on the Acropolis.

Athena was a lovely maiden, taller and more beautiful than any human maid. She wore helmet and breastplate, because when Athenians went to war she always went with them and fought for them. She had grey eyes and the kindest smile in the world.

If you were in trouble Athena might put on her sandals, which never grew old, and come flying through the air to help you. You probably would not recognize her. You would think she was some good friend you knew. You would talk with her and she would advise you and help you. Then all of a sudden 'your friend' would be wrapped in a cloud or a rosy mist, and so would disappear. Then you would know you had seen Athena.

All this Theras believed. But you must not think him foolish for so believing. Athena was his goddess. The wise, grown-up men in Athens believed in her, respected her, and loved her.

And often they prayed to Athena so truly and thought her so good and kind that their prayers reached to the true God over all.

When Theras went up on the Acropolis he was in Athena's home. No wonder he thought the tall brazen goddess was Athena herself.

Theras and Pheidon walked past the many statues of gods, and warriors and heroes, statues of boys who had won prizes for running or throwing the disc. They were all painted so that

THE ACROPOLIS

they looked alive. Pheidon and Theras walked straight to the Parthenon, Athena's beautiful temple, for Pheidon must now thank the goddess for bringing his ship back home.

The temple door was to the east, so that the sun could shine in the moment it arose over the mountain. The sun was shining into it now.

Theras caught a gleam and glitter of gold.

'What is it?' he whispered.

Pheidon took his hand and answered in a low, solemn voice: 'It is the new image of Athena, the one Pheidias made.'

They stepped into the lovely temple. The sunlight from behind them fell straight upon the breast of the image and from there shone in a golden mist upon the face—such a great *thinking* face! It was just the colour of little Opis's[1] face, awakening rosy from sleep. The goddess's grey eyes looked down into Theras's eyes as though she were loving him, really noticing him, and at the same time dreaming about heaven.

'Has she had a dream?' whispered Theras.

[1] Opis was Theras' baby sister.

30

The Parthenon

GREEK ORDERS OF ARCHITECTURE

A Greek temple was built in one of three orders (styles) of architecture. The main differences between them are shown in the drawings. All columns are fluted (grooved) and the different surfaces of the temple were brightly coloured, with red and blue predominating. Reading from left to right:

1. The Doric order was the earliest and simplest. There was no base to the column which was broad compared to those of the other orders (its height was 5 or 6 times its width). The columns were bridged by the architrave, above which was the entablature consisting of alternate triglyphs (stones with three grooves) and metopes (square blocks decorated with sculpture in relief).
2. The column of the Ionic order was more slender (its height was 9 times its width). It was more decorative at the base of the column, with scrolls at the top. The sculpture on the entablature formed a continuous frieze.
3. The Corinthian order was like the Ionic but had a decoration of acanthus leaves in an inverted bell shape at the top of the column.

Every year the Athenians held a festival called the Panathenaea in honour of Athene: a grand procession went up to the Parthenon, with the offering of a robe for Athene. The sculptor Pheidias carved the procession on the frieze of the Parthenon, and these sculptures survive to this day. They are in the British Museum and are known as the Elgin marbles because

Lord Elgin acquired them for Britain in the early nineteenth century.

However, Sparta's fears and jealousy increased and the Athenians grew more ambitious and overbearing. War broke out between them again in 431 B.C. It was called the Peloponnesian War because Athens' opponents were Sparta and her allies in the southern part of Greece called the Peloponnese. A year after the war started a plague broke out at Athens. Thucydides was an Athenian historian who caught the plague but lived to write the description which follows.

The Plague

That year, as is generally admitted, was particularly free from all other kinds of illness, though those who did have any illness previously all caught the plague in the end. In other cases, however, there seemed to be no reason for the attacks. People in perfect health suddenly began to have burning feelings in the head; their eyes became red and inflamed; inside their mouths there was bleeding from the throat and tongue, and the breath became unnatural and unpleasant. The next symptoms were sneezing and hoarseness of voice, and before long the pain settled on the chest and was accompanied by coughing. Next the stomach was affected with stomach-aches and with vomitings of every kind of bile that has been given a name by the medical profession, all this being accompanied by great pain and difficulty. In most cases there were attacks of ineffectual retching, producing violent spasms; this sometimes ended with this stage of the disease, but sometimes continued long afterwards. Externally the body was not very hot to the touch, nor was there any pallor: the skin was rather reddish and livid, breaking out into small pustules and ulcers. But inside there was a feeling of burning, so that people could not bear the touch even of the lightest linen clothing, but wanted to be completely naked, and indeed most of all would have liked to plunge into cold water. Many of the sick who were uncared for actually did so, plunging into the water-tanks in an effort to relieve a thirst which was unquenchable; for it was just the same with them whether they drank much or little.

Then all the time they were afflicted with insomnia and the desperate feeling of not being able to keep still.

In the period when the disease was at its height, the body, so far from wasting away, showed surprising powers of resistance to all the agony, so that there was still some strength left on the seventh or eighth day, which was the time when, in most cases, death came from the internal fever. But if people survived this critical period, then the disease descended to the bowels, producing violent ulceration and uncontrollable diarrhoea, so that most of them died later as a result of the weakness caused by this. For the disease, first settling in the head, went on to affect every part of the body in turn, and even when people escaped its worst effects, it still left its traces on them by fastening upon the extremities of the body. It affected the fingers, and the toes, and many of those who recovered lost the use of these members; some, too, went blind. There were some also who, when they first began to get better, suffered from a total loss of memory, not knowing who they were themselves and being unable to recognize their friends.

Thucydides was the first historian who considered it most important to find out exactly what had happened and record the truth. In fact doctors following his description of the disease have recognized it as typhus.

The Athenians were completely demoralized by the plague. Thousands of them had prayed to the gods that they might recover from the disease but the gods had not answered their prayers. These Athenians and many others came to believe that the Olympian gods had no power or did not even exist.[1] In addition to this the Athenians lost a third of their population, including Pericles, their leader, who had managed their affairs almost continuously for fifteen years.

The war dragged on for ten years until the two sides made peace. A few years later however, war broke out again when a young Athenian called Alcibiades had the idea of sending an expedition to Sicily: after conquering Syracuse, the chief city there, Athens would use her fleet to conquer Carthage, the largest

[1] Like the schoolmaster on pp. 37–39.

33

trading city in the Mediterranean, and then strengthened by both these enemy fleets she would return to Greece and destroy the Spartans. This was Alcibiades' plan, but before it could be carried out it had to be approved by the Athenian people in an Assembly.[1] The following story is told by a young Athenian who goes with his grandfather to the Assembly to hear Alcibiades and Nicias argue about whether an expedition should be sent.

The Assembly

But this was one of the occasions when the respectable element wasn't having it all its own way. Speaker after speaker got up to commend the Sicilian project. The infection by this time had spread to all ages and all classes. All were convinced the expedition would be invincible. Men with grey in their beards said boisterously the question was not whether the expedition would prove a success, but how soon. People of Alcibiades' age talked largely of being 'cooped up' in Athens. Poorer people as well as the traders saw in the idea a heaven-sent chance of getting rich quickly. Rowers, it had been proposed, would get far more than the usual rate of pay; already people were discussing what should be done with the tribute gained from the rich Sicilian cities. And finally, after his cronies had carefully built up an atmosphere for him, Alcibiades himself spoke.

Anyone being told years later exactly what he said on this occasion, may well ask in amazement, 'How did he get away with it?' for he really made no attempt to meet the points raised by Nicias. But you would ask this only if you had never known Alcibiades. Nicias had the good arguments, a wretched voice, a distinctly uncharming physical appearance; Alcibiades, having a magnificent voice and splendid looks did not have to bother with arguments.

What exactly did he say?

That he deserved to command because of what he had done in the Olympics. By entering seven teams—a number never entered before by any person—which came first, second and

[1] For some more information about how the Athenian democracy worked see suggested activity for finding out (6) on p. 41.

34

fourth, and taking good care that it was all done in great style, he had entirely confounded those who thought Athens was ruined by the war; indeed, he had made such a magnificent impression that people now thought us to be more powerful than we actually were. The same applied to his general style of living. At this there was a growl from Grandfather, 'So because he has a silk bedspread, they're shivering in their shoes in Sparta?'

And then he fell to baiting the wretched Nicias, playing on his hatred of being left out in the cold. Nicias felt he was too young, he said; Nicias himself was no longer young, but was notorious for his luck. Let Athens, therefore, make use both of his own youth and Nicias' luck, and elect them both.

So the cracked voice of Nicias was heard again, and his tactics were soon obvious. He meant to chill his hearers' blood by emphasizing the enormous difficulties of the expedition, after which he calculated the Assembly would conclude the enterprise was not worth the effort; he therefore demanded an enormous force of a hundred triremes, soldiers and supplies, five thousand heavy infantry, archers, slingers—oh, yes, and grain and bakers—which made my family promptly conclude as one man that he'd cornered the market in wheat and barley. He was promptly voted them.

Grandfather looked without pity at his dropped jaw, his face grey with consternation, and said, 'Now he realizes he's given Alcibiades the biggest expedition ever to sail from Greece.'

I regret that he was unkind enough to push through the excited crowd and say as much to Nicias, as the Assembly broke up. Nicias looked at him with acute dislike, and said, 'Alcibiades doesn't have sole command, you know.'

'If that expedition sails, he'll be in charge all right.'

Nicias glared.

The Sicilian expedition failed disastrously. Alcibiades was recalled when the fleet was on its way; Nicias fell ill, and was killed together with most of the army, and a relief expedition sent out to help him. Athens never completely recovered and finally surrendered to the Spartans in 404 B.C.

Athens was defeated mainly because of the bad decisions that were made on occasions like the debate between Alcibiades and

Nicias. Yet the Athenian system of government was very just and well organized. A general or unjust official could be brought before the law-courts, and the system was carefully organized so that justice might be done and be seen to be done. In the following story Alexis and Theo, two Athenian boys, go with their father to a law-court. They take a friend, Lucian, with them.

Gentlemen of the Jury

'You must miss your class with Milon tomorrow morning,' said Father at supper.

'Oh, yes, Father. Why?' he said readily.

'I'm taking you to the law-court. It's good for a boy to go now and again, and see how things are run. Lucian's coming with us. His father may be on the jury, so I said I'd look after him.'

'Good! That'll be interesting. What's the case, Father?'

'Alleged blasphemy.'

'What's alleged blasphemy?' demanded Theo. He spoke the last word with gusto, enjoying the explosive sound.

'Blasphemy means speaking or acting disrespectfully to the gods. Alleged means they *say* the man did it, but they must prove it before he can be punished.'

Alexis had gone pale, and when he spoke he found it hard to keep his voice casual. 'Who is it, Father?' He was relieved when Father named someone he had never heard of.[1]

'Should be an interesting case,' said Father. 'Very seldom it comes up. Must be years since there was one quite like this. Maybe it's a pity,' he added darkly, 'that it doesn't come up a little oftener.'

They started for the market-place straight after breakfast, and found a big crowd assembling, most of the five thousand men whose names were on the jurors' register for the year.

'They're divided into ten lists, five hundred each,' Father explained. 'Nobody knows till the morning of the trial which five hundred will serve on the jury—the officials are drawing lots now to decide.'

'What a waste of time, making everybody turn up!'

[1] Alexis was afraid that Socrates, a great friend of his, was on trial.

'There's a reason. By leaving it to the last moment, they make it impossible to get at the jury and bribe them.'

Alexis thought for a moment, then asked in a quiet tone which had a faint echo of Socrates: 'Wouldn't it be better to find a jury of honest men who could be relied on not to take bribes?'

'Much better,' Father agreed, 'but much harder!'

At that moment there was a hush while the herald gave out which jury was to serve, and then a general movement as the others went about their business and the chosen jurymen lined up to get their coloured sticks of office and their tickets, entitling them to a day's pay at the end of the trial.

'It *is* the panel that my father's on,' said Lucian, rather pleased. 'Come on, sir, they always try their cases in the Middle Court. Let's get good places up against the rail.'

It was another half-hour before all the preliminaries were over, the sacrifices offered to the gods, the jury settled on their mat-covered benches, the general public herded behind the rail by the police, and the president enthroned on his platform, between two lower platforms from which the prosecutor and the defendant would speak.

'That box the clerk is opening contains the charge and the evidence,' Father whispered. 'The papers in the case have been sealed up ever since the first private hearing. They call the box the "hedgehog".'

'Why?'

'No idea,' Father admitted. 'Just an old name.'

'I'll ask my father tonight,' said Lucian. 'I should think *he'd* know.'

The case began. Alexis was glad to find that, though Father might not know why the sealed box was nicknamed the hedgehog, he was well up in all the other details of the law. His whispered explanations made everything clear, and he was able to answer all the questions the boys put to him.

Alexis found himself even more interested in the subject of the case than in the procedure for trying it. The accused was a schoolmaster, charged with teaching his boys that the sun was not really a god, Apollo, driving a flaming chariot across the sky, but an enormous mass of white-hot matter, almost as large as Greece. Nor was the moon a goddess, Apollo's sister

Artemis, but another lifeless mineral body, shining by reflection of the sun.

'He must be crazy,' Lucian hissed. 'Can you imagine such nonsense?'

'Crazy to teach it in a school, maybe,' Alexis agreed. 'Maybe not so crazy to believe it himself!' He took care not to let Father catch the last remark. Lucian's shocked expression was quite enough.

When the schoolmaster stood up to make his defence, he denied teaching his class that these theories were true. He had mentioned them, certainly. He believed that boys should be trained to think for themselves, and to distinguish between the right and the wrong. After all, he was not the first to bring forward the theories—anyone was free to buy the books of Anaxagoras the philosopher, in which they were fully discussed.

There was a hostile murmur from the jury. In the circumstances, the mention of Anaxagoras was tactless, '*He* was exiled for these theories when I was a young man,' Father explained. 'It caused a stir, because he was a friend of Pericles, but even Pericles couldn't save him.'

The case ended. The jury filed past the voting urns. Each man had two tokens, one for 'guilty' and the other for 'not guilty'. He dropped the one he wished to use into the first urn. The waste tokens clinked into the other.

The result was 'guilty', by a large majority. The prosecutor then demanded a sentence of exile. The schoolmaster, supported by his wife and three children, all in their oldest clothes and weeping to win sympathy, begged the jury to let him off with a heavy fine.

'Why doesn't he suggest a smaller one?' asked Lucian.

'Well, the jury have got to choose one penalty or the other —they can't fix it themselves.'

'I see. If he said too little, then, they'd be sure to vote for exile?'

'Exactly.'

Alexis was relieved when the result of the second vote was announced. The schoolmaster was to be fined. 'But of course,' said Lucian, 'his school will be ruined—no one'll send their kids to a bounder like that.'

Outside the court they met Lucian's father. He said he had voted with the more merciful majority. 'You see,' he told his indignant son, 'this schoolmaster fellow is only small fry, really. The case was no more than a try-out, just to test public opinion.'

'Do you mean, sir,' said Alexis with sinking heart, 'that they'll be bringing more cases? Against—against other people?'

'Well, it's high time we did, my boy. You youngsters have got to be protected. And there's far too much dangerous nonsense talked nowadays. Free speech is all very well, but . . .' He shrugged his shoulders. 'One has to go carefully in these matters. It's so different from an ordinary criminal case. Depends more on public opinion, and that's apt to shift from month to month. When we go after the really dangerous fellows, we need to be quite sure of a conviction. They're tricky customers, and if they got acquitted it would do far more harm than if they'd been let alone in the first place.'

'Let's hope this case will be a warning,' said Father. 'I don't *like* interfering with any man's liberty to speak his mind——'

'There'll be some more cases all right in due time,' Lucian's father assured them. 'Some people are just waiting to have a crack at these clever fellows.' He was almost smacking his lips at the thought. Alexis saw in his mind's eye a sickening vision of Socrates standing up to face five hundred 'gentlemen of the jury' as self-satisfied and prejudiced and deaf to new ideas as Lucian's father. Socrates would never cringe and beg for mercy. If he ever came to be sentenced it would be exile at least, more likely death.

However, in spite of these faults we still consider the jury system the fairest way of getting justice done and a democracy the fairest way of governing a country. And it was the Athenians who first realized this.

Suggested Activities

Writing

1. Imagine you were a Spartan visiting Athens for the first time and writing a letter home describing what you saw and

did. You would probably have been to the Parthenon, the Assembly and the Law Courts at least.

2. Write the diary of someone who caught the plague, and survived.

3. An Athenian's way of life was completely different from a Spartan's (see pp. 3–4, C. D. Snedeker, *Theras*, and Rosemary Sutcliff, *The Truce of the Games*). Which would you prefer to be? Write as if you were a Spartan or an Athenian claiming that your way of life was the best.

4. Describe how *you* won the foot race or some other event in the Ancient Olympic Games. See pp. 23 to 26. Besides the race itself you could mention the training, the moments before the race, the prize (Was it worth it?) and your reception when you got home.

Drawing

1. Make a drawing of the three orders of Greek columns. You could colour them as the Greeks originally did this. They probably used red, blue and gold to emphasize the lines of the columns and their decorations.

2. Make up and draw your own order.

3. Draw a poster or produce a brochure advertising the attractions of Ancient Athens. Make the Parthenon the centre piece of your drawing.

4. Every year the Athenians held the Panathenaea, a festival in honour of Athene. On the last day of the festival there was a magnificent procession in which a robe specially woven for her and embroidered with a picture of the fight between Athene and the giants was carried to her temple. The robe was carried on a great ship on wheels followed by girls carrying baskets with the tools of sacrifice, by boys carrying bowls, old men with olive branches, chariots and young men on horseback.

Draw a picture of the procession. (It is also shown on the frieze of the Parthenon—see p. 31.)

5. Draw a time-line from 500 B.C. to 400 B.C. marking in the most important events. One line for every five years would give you the right spacing.

Suggested Activities

Acting

1. Stage a debate between an Athenian and a Spartan arguing that their way of life was the best (see also *Writing* 3).

2. Make a series of interviews as if for radio during the plague at Athens. Some could imagine that they had caught the plague and survived, and others that they had lived through the time.

3. Stage the trial, Athenian fashion, of the schoolmaster who taught his boys that the sun was an enormous mass of white-hot matter almost as large as Greece.

Finding Out

1. Find examples of Greek orders in the buildings of your own town and make sketches of them. See which order they belong to and whether they are exactly like the originals.

2. Find out about other Greek temples and temples of other peoples. (Look up: temples, Egypt, Rome, architecture, etc.)

3. Find illustrations of other Greek statues or pictures on Greek pottery and copy them.

4. What other Gods and Goddesses did the ancient Greeks worship? Make a list of their Greek and Roman names and the work each of them did. (See the companion volume, *Gods and Heroes of Ancient Greece*, pp. 111–112.)

5. What other events were there in the ancient Olympic Games? Describe how they were staged. How many of these are still in the modern Olympic Games? List in three columns those events which were only held in the ancient games, those held only in the modern games and those held in both. Write a short history of both games (for the origins of the games see pp. 16–21 in the companion volume *Gods and Heroes of Ancient Greece*).

6. Athens was the first democracy. Democracy is a Greek word meaning 'power of the people' and means that the people as a whole, not a king or part of the nation, have the power of making decisions. Our system of government is a democracy but rather different to the Athenian form of democracy. In Athens, if an important decision had to be made, the whole people would gather together in an Assembly to discuss the problem and vote. This was possible because there were only

about 50,000 Athenians who could vote (women, children, slaves and foreigners were not allowed) and they all lived in the state of Attica, the country surrounding Athens with no part more than 30 miles away from it. So everyone in Attica could get in to Athens on important occasions to vote.

Find out the differences between this and our system. Which do you think is better?

7. Find out the differences between the Athenian way of staging a trial and ours. Do you think that either are better than the other in any way?

8. Find out more about Socrates who was sentenced to death although he above all tried to obey the laws and do what was right.

Further Reading
R. L. Green, *Ancient Greece*, Young Historian series.
R. L. Green, *A True Book about Ancient Greece*.
H. and R. Leacroft, *The Buildings of Ancient Athens*.
Stephanie Plowman, *The Road to Sardis*.
C. D. Snedeker, *Theras: The Story of an Athenian Boy*.
Rosemary Sutcliff, *The Truce of the Games*.
Geoffrey Trease, *The Crown of Violet*.
E. J. Sheppard, *Ancient Athens*, Then and There series.

3 Alexander the Great

Alexander was the son of King Philip of Macedon. Macedon was a country to the north of Greece, looked upon by the Greeks as half Greek, half barbarian. King Philip had Alexander taught by the wisest man of his time, the 'master of those that know', the Greek writer and thinker Aristotle. As well as being clever and well educated, Alexander excelled in strength and courage. One day when a horse dealer came to Pella, the capital of Macedon, Alexander went with his cousin Herakleides to inspect the horses.

Ox-Blaze

In a little while they all went down to the field to look at the horses, first the replacements for the army and then the others. These Thessalian horses stood fairly high, a different breed from the stubby chariot horses or the hog-maned ponies that carry through all eternity the young Athenian knights in the Parthenon frieze. But an armoured rider with a heavy lance and a peaked war saddle needs a strong, big-boned horse. Suddenly Herakleides nudged Alexander. 'Look!'

Two of the grooms were leading out another horse, a high-stepping young horse, a bay with a white blaze very clear on his forehead and very like the kind of blaze you often saw on the red-brown plough oxen. The horse whinnied and then gave a sideways jump, more than a shy, which nearly took the grooms off their feet. But Philonikos shouted at them angrily to run. The horse broke into a trot, almost quietly for a minute and with a lovely movement. Then quite suddenly went into a canter that changed into a breathtaking gallop and shed the two grooms as though they had been flies.

Alexander gave a gasp of pleasure and suddenly knew this was the horse he wanted.

THE EMPIRE OF ALEXANDER THE GREAT
(Notice how small Rome's territory was at the time)

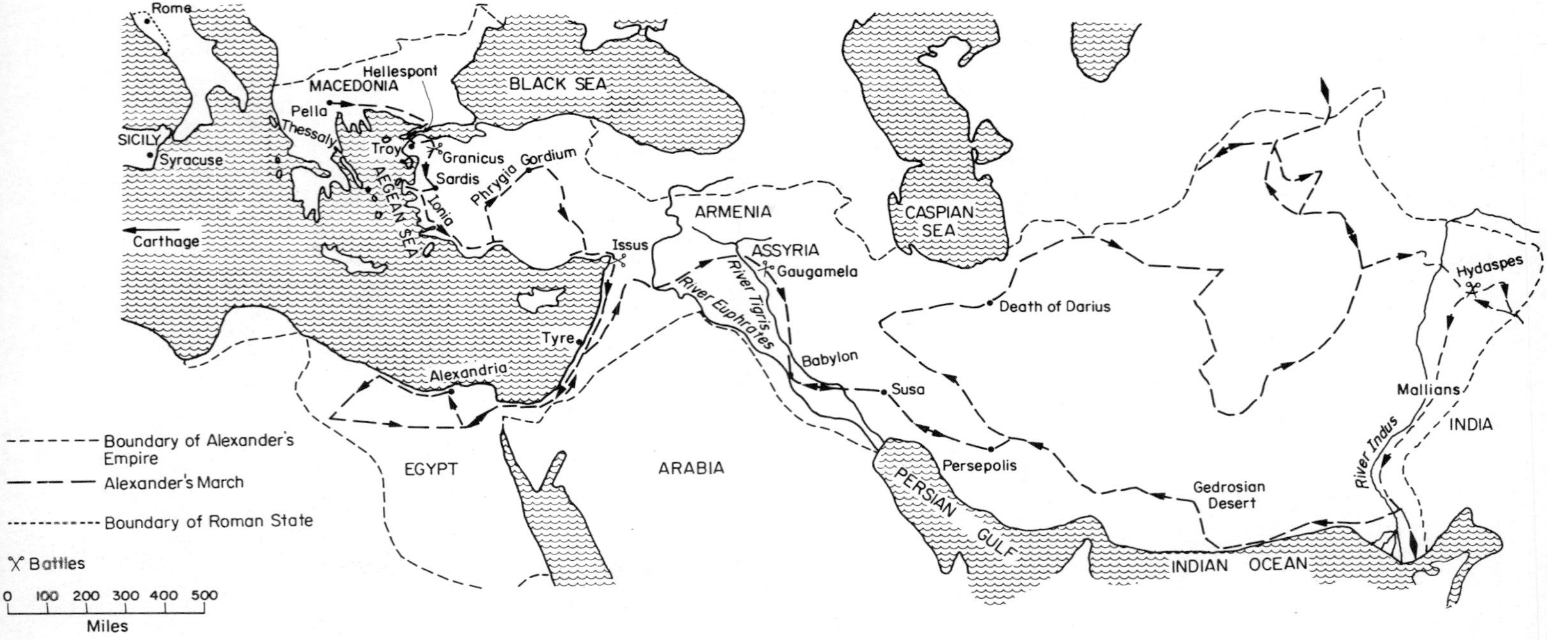

Miles

0   100   200   300   400   500

- - - - - Boundary of Alexander's Empire
━━━━━ Alexander's March
.... Boundary of Roman State
✕ Battles

Roma
SICILY
Syracuse
Carthage
MACEDONIA
Pella
Thessaly
Hellespont
Troy
Granicus
Gordium
Phrygia
Sardis
Ionia
AEGEAN SEA
BLACK SEA
Issus
Tyre
Alexandria
EGYPT
ARABIA
ARMENIA
ASSYRIA
Gaugamela
River Tigris
River Euphrates
Babylon
Susa
CASPIAN SEA
Death of Darius
Persepolis
PERSIAN GULF
Gedrosian Desert
INDIAN OCEAN
INDIA
River Indus
Mallians
Hydaspes

ALEXANDER THE GREAT

'That Ox-Blaze!' said Philonikos. 'Showing off!' and swore
at him copiously.

The ring of watchers round the field turned the horse, who,
however, went through all kinds of games, rearing and lashing
out and refusing to be touched. Herakleides went confidently
in to handle him but was extremely put out when the horse

first shied away like a wild creature, then wheeled round ready to kick and showing the whites of his eyes. In fact he was both put out and disappointed, for certainly this was a magnificent horse, fit for a king. Fit above all for a strong man in full armour, for this horse would carry him a hand's-breadth higher, that most important hand's breadth that just gives the extra thrust on the killing lancepoint! You couldn't fault him. Wonderful legs and chest, but what a devil!

'Something scared him,' said Philonikos, 'but I know what he's worth and I'm not taking a penny off the price, King Philip!'

Herakleides came back, shaking his head. 'What's the use, he's unbroken and too old to handle.'

Oh no, thought Alexander, he's mine!

'He's nervous,' said Philonikos, 'not used to kings, what? Let him settle down.' The horse dropped his head, took a nibble of grass but kept a wary eye open, moving away if anyone came up on his quarters. Finally he managed to kick one of Philonikos' men head over heels.

Herakleides was scowling and shook his head at the King. 'Useless!' he said. 'What's more, that horse'll kill someone before he's done. Besides, look at the price they're asking for him!'

'I think he's worth it!' said Alexander suddenly.

Philonikos had overheard the last few words. 'Don't you worry—I'll get the price from someone that *knows* about horses.'

King Philip turned his back angrily. 'Utter nonsense!' he said. 'That horse will never be schooled.'

He was walking away but Alexander was jumping from foot to foot. 'They're all fools!' he shouted and he suddenly felt that the horse—*his* horse!—was being stolen from him. 'I'll take him on. I'll ride him! Father, let's have a bet on it!'

The King stopped abruptly. 'You look exactly like your mother,' he said disapprovingly.

But Alexander didn't care. 'They're throwing him away!' he cried passionately. 'That lovely horse—my horse! Father, take me on—I'll pay you his price if I don't master him!' Suddenly he saw Aristotle behind his father, worried, watching his pupil get out of control into one of his rages and, all at once, he found he had taken a deep breath, was smiling and speaking courteously and gently. 'I believe I know how to do it. My Lord Father, trust me with the horse.'

Philip looked at him. 'All right,' he said. 'Try it, and I'll keep you to your bet.'

Herakleides had grabbed the King by the arm, trying to stop him, but Alexander took off his cloak and walked slowly out towards the horse, talking to him, calling him by his nickname of Ox-Blaze. The horse lifted his head and watched him, turning a little. Still talking to him, Alexander walked round a few yards across the field until he had the horse facing directly into the sun. He had noticed that not only did the horse dislike things like flapping cloaks, but he hated people coming up on his flanks, and especially their tricky little shadows. Even his own shadow worried him. A direct and quiet approach might work. Alexander stood still, whispering to Ox-Blaze, while the tall horse snuffed at him, first his chest, then his open mouth. Horse lips nibbled at him. He raised his hand gently.

The bridle was still on the horse's head, the reins lying loose on his neck. Alexander moved to the reins but the horse did not seem to bother. Then Alexander bent his knees and leaped straight from the ground on to the horse's back. Ox-Blaze tossed his head and looked round, but his rider did not pull at the reins, only went on talking to him and stroking him down with a firm hand. The horse moved on a step or two; Alexander did not interfere, beyond keeping him facing into the sun. He knew that his father was watching and the Companions and Aristotle. But he was not thinking of that, only of keeping up this confident and happy relation with Ox-Blaze.

Then he began to encourage him a little with knees and heels, speaking louder. The horse's ears went back, but to listen, not in anger. His pace quickened. 'Go on!' said Alexander. 'Faster, my love, my beauty, faster!' and then in three great bounds Ox-Blaze was stretched in a tearing all-out gallop, away, away! Alexander shouted to them at the end of the field to give him room and they backed away hastily. There was a low stone dyke which the horse cleared without a pause, shooting up, his legs gathered, and then violently stretched; after that another field. Another jump and Alexander and the horse were far and small. Was the horse bolting or was it possible that the crouched rider was in control?

ALEXANDER ON BUCEPHALUS

King Philip stood very still, his hand up to his mouth. Half
turning, he saw his son's tutor. 'I should never have let him do
it,' he said. 'That devil will kill him, and it will be my fault!'
and there was no answer Aristotle could make. None, none!
Only that he too loved the boy.

Then beside them Ptolemy yelled: 'Look, look!' for the

horse had turned, was tearing back at the same gallop, but the rider was still on him, was beginning to sit up, to gather in the reins—'Alexander, Alexander!' they were all shouting. 'Victory, victory!' And his father too was shouting at the top of his voice, with the tears streaming down his face.

But by the time Alexander had brought Ox-Blaze to a canter, a trot, a quiet walk, the King was himself again. Alexander slid off in front of his father, but did not give the reins up till he had made much of the horse, petting him, pulling his ears gently, rubbing his own face against the horse's muzzle until they each had the smell of the other. The horse was in a lather but not badly blown. Herakleides took the bridle and Ox-Blaze jerked his head up crossly but Alexander came back, talked to him, patted him again and left him quiet, one ear pricked forward to listen to the voice which had now become part of his life.

Alexander was all over horse, face, arms and legs smeared with lather, his short tunic the same. But his father took him by the ears and kissed him. 'You did it,' he said.

'Yes,' said Alexander. 'My horse, Father?'

King Philip turned to the Thessalian. 'I'll give you the price you ask, Philonikos. But mind this! If that Ox-Blaze of yours had killed my son I'd have had you crucified.'

'But he didn't,' said Alexander. 'He didn't want to—not with me.'

'What are you going to call him, son?' the King asked.

'I think I shall go on calling him Bucephalus—Ox-Blaze. It's the name I called him at our first meeting.'

'But that's not a noble name!'

'He will make it noble. I know. Look at him.' But everyone was looking at him. 'Did you think he was going to kill me?' Alexander said to his tutor. 'Would you have minded?'

'Very much,' said Aristotle. 'As you understand well, Alexander. But this time you knew better than any of us. So I suppose this horse of yours will be coming to my lectures?'

'Almost,' said Alexander, 'almost!' and went back to the horse who reached out his head towards him at once.

Alexander, like every well-educated Greek, would know by heart Homer's two great poems about the Trojan War The

49

Iliad *and* The Odyssey *often called 'the bible of the Greeks'.
Alexander hero-worshipped Achilles, the greatest Greek fighter
in the Trojan War. Like him he determined to avenge himself
on someone from the East who had wronged Greece. Achilles'
enemy had been Paris; Alexander's enemy was Darius, a descendant of the Darius who had sent the force to fight against Athens
at Marathon 150 years before Alexander's time. Ever since then
Greeks had dreamt of avenging the injuries they had suffered
during the Persian Wars, but no one had the strength or confidence. Alexander had the strength: his father had built up a
well-trained and practised army as all through his reign he had
fought against enemies surrounding Macedon and later in
Greece. Alexander also had confidence: his father had given him
a good training during these wars in the skills of fighting and
leading an army.*

*When Philip died he had defeated all his enemies in Greece in-
cluding Athens which had become a second-rate power after being
defeated by Sparta in the Peloponnesian War. So Alexander
was free to attack the one remaining enemy, Persia. In 334 B.C.
he crossed his army over the Hellespont, as the Persian King
Xerxes had done 146 years before when going the opposite way
to attack Greece. His army numbered 40,000 men, but the
Persians could raise armies of hundreds of thousands of men and
Persia was a hundred times the size of Macedon. After making a
sacrifice at Achilles' tomb at Troy, Alexander joined battle with
the Persians at the River Granicus nearby and gained a quick
victory. As always Alexander fought in the thick of the battle,
and was nearly killed: a Persian got behind him with axe raised
to strike when Kleitas, Alexander's friend, in the nick of time
struck him on the shoulder, severing his arm.*

The Gordian Knot

At about this time Alexander penetrated into the kingdom of
Phrygia, and crossed over the River Marsyas to occupy
Gordium. This city was the former capital of the country, and
had taken its name from King Gordus, the founder.

Macedonian forces met scarcely any resistance. Soon after
he had made his entry into the conquered town, Alexander

The Gordian Knot

followed his usual custom and set out to visit the shrines of the local gods. The priests received him with great respect. One of them took the young king to see the sights of the city, ending up at the temple of Zeus. Here he was shown the ancient chariot of King Gordus. It was no longer in a condition to be used; all that was left was the shaft and the yoke. These two pieces of wood were tied together by an extraordinary tangle of cords and knots.

When Alexander came nearer to inspect this strange relic, the high priest told him that an oracle had declared that the domination of the whole of Asia would be assured to the man who could undo this knot.

Without thinking, Alexander, who was incapable of resisting a challenge, began to try to loosen the rope from the yoke. He examined the ravelling of the cords, and tried to follow the tangle of the strands, but each time his eyes or his fingers failed him.

His movements were watched breathlessly by the spectators. The Phrygians hoped secretly that the king would be unsuccessful. The Macedonians were anxious, and critical of Alexander for having light-heartedly accepted such a challenge.

A quarter of an hour passed while Alexander displayed unusual patience in trying to solve the problem before him. A second quarter of an hour of tense anxiety followed. The knot was as strong as ever; Alexander had not even found the end of the cord.

The situation was becoming very serious. On every side, faces began to show signs of strain. Even the high priest began to regret that he had ever told the story of the oracle.

Finally, after one last attempt, Alexander looked up. He gazed around him and saw both the anxious faces of the Macedonians and the smug and satisfied expression of the Phrygians. Suddenly, he realized that he had come to a dead end. He understood that his prestige was at stake. Clearly, he would have to bring the whole affair to a satisfactory conclusion.

Alexander then grasped the hilt of his sword, drew it out with a flourish and, with a single blow, cut the knot.

The yoke, released from the rope, fell noisily on to the flagstones with a crash which broke the ominous silence.

Alexander the Great

Immediately, Alexander turned towards his friends and said in a calm voice, 'It is done.'

Then, looking at the priest, he added, 'The oracle did not say *how* the knot was to be undone.'

Alexander marched with all speed through Asia Minor and as he turned south to march along the eastern coast of the Mediterranean was met by Darius with an army twice the size of his own. In the battle which followed at Issus, Alexander defeated Darius, who fled from the battle, and took his queen, mother and daughters captive. He then had a difficult decision to make. Should he pursue Darius inland, thus leaving a large part of his empire unconquered behind him and allowing Darius to raise another army, or should he conquer the eastern coast of the Mediterranean and Egypt first, and then pursue Darius? Alexander chose the slower but surer plan and marched down the coast. First he had to conquer the Phoenician city of Tyre. It had a strong fleet and was built on an island half a mile from the coast. Alexander had no fleet and it took him seven whole months to capture the city. Another few months and he had conquered and organized the country of Egypt. Here he founded Alexandria, one of the many cities to bear his name throughout the East. As Alexander intended, for many centuries it helped to spread Greek ideas and safeguarded Egypt; for well over 2,000 years it has been a great seaport and encouraged trade.

Alexander retraced his steps by way of Tyre and advanced towards the heart of the Persian empire, down the valley of the river Tigris. Here at Gaugamela he was met by Darius with a Persian army so vast that the Greeks at first despaired. Alexander rejected the idea of a night attack as he did not want to steal a victory, and slept so soundly that his generals had to wake him up for battle. Alexander's army was far outflanked by the enemy, but he pretended to attack to the right and then drove straight at the centre of the Persian army where Darius was stationed. As Alexander came close Darius panicked. He fled and the rest of the Persian army followed. The immediate prize of the battle was the wealthiest city of the ancient world, Babylon.

Babylon

Babylon lies in a wide plain, a vast city in the form of a square with sides nearly fourteen miles long and a circuit of some fifty-six miles, and in addition to its enormous size it surpasses in splendour any city of the known world. It is surrounded by a broad deep moat full of water, and within the moat there is a wall fifty royal cubits wide and two hundred high (the royal cubit is two inches longer than the ordinary cubit). And now I must describe how the soil dug out to make the moat was used, and the method of building the wall. While the digging was going on, the earth that was shovelled out was formed into bricks, which were baked in ovens as soon as a sufficient number were made; then using hot bitumen for mortar the workmen began by building parapets along each side of the moat, and then went on to erect the actual wall. In both cases they laid rush-mats between every thirty courses of brick. On the top of the wall they constructed, along each edge, a row of one-roomed buildings facing inwards with enough space between for a four-horse chariot to turn. There are a hundred gates in the circuit of the wall, all of bronze with bronze uprights and lintels.

A RECONSTRUCTION OF BABYLON

The Euphrates, a broad, deep, swift river which rises in Armenia and flows into the Persian Gulf, runs through the middle of the city and divides it in two. The wall is brought right down to the water on both sides, and at an angle to it there is another wall on each bank, built of baked bricks without mortar, running through the town. There are a great many houses of three and four stories. The main streets and the side streets which lead to the river are all dead straight, and for every one of the side streets or alleys there was a bronze gate in the river wall by which the water could be reached.

The great wall I have described is, so to speak, the breast-plate or chief defence of the city; but there is a second one within it, not so thick but hardly less strong. There is a fortress in the middle of each half of the city: in one the royal palace surrounded by a wall of great strength, in the other the temple of Bel, the Babylonian Zeus. The temple is a square building, two furlongs each way, with bronze gates, and was still in existence in my time; it has a solid central tower, one furlong square, with a second erected on top of it and then a third, and so on up to eight. All eight towers can be climbed by a spiral way running round the outside, and about half way up there are seats for those who make the ascent to rest on. On the summit of the topmost tower stands a great temple with a fine large couch in it, richly covered, and a golden table beside it.

In the temple of Babylon there is a second shrine lower down, in which is a great sitting figure of Bel, all of gold on a golden throne, supported on a base of gold, with a golden table standing beside it. I was told by the Chaldaeans that, to make all this, more than twenty-two tons of gold were used. Outside the temple is a golden altar, and there is another one, not of gold, but of great size, on which sheep are sacrificed. The golden altar is reserved for the sacrifice of sucklings only. Again, on the larger altar the Chaldaeans offer something like two and a half tons of frankincense every year at the festival of Bel.

Alexander could not delay: Darius was still free, and while he could he pressed on and took the two capital cities of the empire—Susa and Persepolis. He rested the winter in the

Persian palaces; his one aim then was to capture Darius. After a furious pursuit Alexander caught up with Darius south of the Caspian Sea, only to find he had been assassinated by a traitor.

Alexander now only had to make sure of the rest of the empire further east. This took him three years' further campaigns. He then marched into India, territory unknown to the Greeks, thought to be the world's end. An Indian prince gathered a large army including elephants and, after a hard fight in which the elephants ran wild, was defeated at the river Hydaspes. Soon after the battle Bucephalus died and Alexander founded a city named after him. But Alexander's men refused to go any farther. Those that were left of the original army had been on the march for eight years and covered thousands of miles. Alexander at first said he would go on without them, and then gave in—his only defeat.

Alexander turned south and entered the territory of the Mallians. They resisted Alexander who tried to storm the town, leading the attack as he had done on scores of other occasions.

Alexander in Peril

The men with the ladders were not quick enough to satisfy Alexander; in his impatience he snatched one from the fellow who carried it and with his own hands reared it against the fortress wall; then, crouched under his shield, up he went. Peucestas followed him with the 'sacred shield'—the shield from the temple of Athene at Troy, which Alexander kept by him and had carried before him in battle. Peucestas was followed by Leonnatus, an officer of the Guard; then Abreas, one of the picked soldiers on double pay, mounted by a second ladder.

The King had now reached the top. Laying his shield on the coping of the wall, he forced some of the defenders back into the fortress, cut down others with his sword, till he stood there on the battlements alone, not one of the enemy within his reach. The sight of him filled the men of the Longshields with terror for his safety; scrambling for precedence, they made a dash for the ladders, but under the excessive load they broke and hurled the climbers to the ground. The rest were helpless.

No Indian ventured to approach Alexander as he stood on the fortress wall; but he was the target of every marksman in the neighbouring towers; men in the town shot at him too— and from no great distance either, as raised ground near the fortress wall brought them within closer range. That it was indeed Alexander who stood there was plain to all: his almost

ALEXANDER IN PERIL

legendary courage no less than his shining armour proclaimed him.

Suddenly a thought crossed his mind: by staying where he was he might well be killed with nothing accomplished; but if he leapt down into the fortress, he might by that very act spread consternation among the enemy, or at least, if it was his fate to die, death would come not without a struggle and as the crown of an exploit which would live upon the lips of men. To think was to act: without further hesitation he made his leap.

Once inside the fortress, he put his back to the wall and made ready to fight. A party of Indians came at him, and he cut them down; their commander rushed forward, all too rashly, and he, too, fell. First one, then a second, who tried to approach him he stopped with a well-aimed stone. Others pressed within striking distance, and fell victims to his sword. After that none ventured again to attack him hand to hand; keeping their distance, they formed a half-circle round where he stood and hurled at him whatever missiles they had or could find.

By this time Peucestas, Abreas, and Leonnatus, the only men who succeeded in scaling the wall before the ladders collapsed, had got inside the fortress and were fighting in defence of their King. Abreas was shot in the face and killed and Alexander himself was hit, the arrow penetrating his corselet and entering his body above the breast. Ptolemy tells us that the blood from the wound was mixed with air breathed out from the pierced lung. Despite the pain he continued to defend himself so long as the blood was warm; but there was soon a violent haemorrhage, as was to be expected with a pierced lung, and overcome by giddiness and faintness he fell forward over his shield. Peucestas stood astride of his body holding up before him the sacred shield from Troy, and Leonnatus took his stand on the other side, both men being now the target for the enemy missiles, while Alexander himself was almost unconscious from loss of blood.

The Macedonian assault upon the fortress was by now thoroughly out of hand; the men had seen Alexander as he stood on the battlements, the mark of the enemy's missiles; they had seen him leap down on the other side; and now, afraid lest his rash act should be the end of him and eager to bring help in time, they made a rush for the fortress wall. The ladders were smashed and useless, but, on the spur of the moment, they used whatever means they could to get up and over: some drove stakes into the clay of the wall and dragged themselves slowly and laboriously up; others struggled by standing on their comrades' shoulders. Each man as he got to the top flung himself down on the further side into the fortress. There they saw the King on the ground, and a cry of grief and a shout of rage rose from every throat. Soon a fierce battle was raging, one man after another holding his shield over Alexander's prostrate body, until at last the troops outside had smashed the bolt of the gate in the curtain-wall and were beginning to come in, a few at a time. Others then got their shoulders to the half-opened gate, forced it inwards, and so laid the fortress open.

Now the slaughter began; neither women nor children were spared. A party of men carried away the King on his shield; his condition was critical and no one, at this time, thought he could live.

After a while he recovered, but a rumour quickly spread to the main part of the army that he had died of his wounds. When Alexander heard this he decided that he must go at once to his men to prove that he was still alive. The troops were in camp at the junction of two rivers, so Alexander sailed downstream to them.

When his vessel had nearly reached them, he ordered the awning over the stern to be taken down so that everyone might see him. Even then the troops were incredulous, and supposed that what they saw on board was Alexander's body. At last, however, the vessel was brought in to the river-bank; Alexander raised a hand in greeting to the men, and immediately there was a shout of joy, and arms were stretched towards him in welcome or lifted to heaven in thankfulness. So unexpected was the sense of relief that many, despite themselves, burst into tears. As he was being moved from the ship, a party of Longshields brought him a stretcher; but he refused it and called for his horse. He mounted, and at the sight of him, once more astride his horse, there was a storm of applause so loud that the river-banks and neighbouring glens re-echoed with the noise. Near his tent he dismounted, and the men saw him walk; they crowded round him, touching his hands, his knees, his clothes; some, content with a sight of him standing near, turned away with a blessing on their lips. Wreaths were flung upon him and such flowers as were then in bloom.

Proceeding further downstream with his army, Alexander reached the River Indus, and then the Indian Ocean. Here Alexander divided his forces: some were to sail back home in a fleet through the Indian Ocean and Persian Gulf; the others marched with Alexander through the Gedrosian Desert. But Alexander for just once in his life had tried to do too much. The army was tormented by thirst; thousands died. Alexander suffered with them: when the only water that could be found one day was brought to him in a helmet, he refused to drink it.

Alexander finally reached the Persian capital Susa, and he set about organizing the countries he had conquered. The empire was so vast that he and the Macedonians could not govern by themselves. Alexander decided to ask the Persians to help in governing the empire. When the Macedonians objected, he took away their positions of authority and gave them to the Persians. The Macedonians begged to be brought into favour again. They were, but did not argue with Alexander after that and the Persians were given a share in the government. Alexander intended that the Greeks and Persians should become one nation. He had married a Persian princess, Roxane, and encouraged his officers and men to take Persian wives.

Alexander now began to make preparations for the invasion and conquest of Arabia. He moved to Babylon, the centre of these preparations and destined to be the capital of his empire. Then he caught a fever and, after twelve days' illness, died. He was aged thirty-two years eight months.

Suggested Activities

Writing

1. List the battles that Alexander won with dates if possible and what he gained by winning the battle.

2. Write a diary as if you were Alexander with a description of the most important or memorable days of your life.

3. Write a diary as if you were one of Alexander's men describing some of the great days of your life. Write what you thought of your leader. Did you admire him, and if so for what?

4. Produce a colour magazine featuring Alexander's life with pictures, maps and articles. You could imagine that it was a special issue brought out when he died.

Alexander the Great

Drawing

1. Draw a picture of Alexander with Bucephalus.
2. Draw a map of the Persian Empire marking in clearly Alexander's march, and another map of Greece marking in Macedon.
3. Draw a series of pictures or a cartoon strip illustrating memorable moments in Alexander's life.
4. Draw a picture of Alexander in battle against King Darius (see p. 56).
5. Draw a map or picture of Babylon using the description on pp. 53–54.

Acting

1. Act the scene when Alexander tries to unravel the Gordian knot.
2. Act as an interviewer of Alexander after one of his victories. Do you think Alexander would be modest or boastful about his victories?
3. A group of you could be Alexander's men trying to persuade him to march no farther, and finally succeeding.

Finding Out

1. How many people have been given the title of 'great'? (For example: Peter, Frederick, Catherine). Find out something about them. What made Alexander *great*? Who do you think was the greatest of all these?
2. Find out how many peoples Alexander conquered.
3. What happened to Alexander's empire after his death?
4. The hanging gardens of Babylon were one of the seven wonders of the Ancient World. Find out what the others were and draw pictures of them, with an explanation of each. Draw a map showing where each of them was. How many of them were in Alexander's Empire?

Further Reading

Hans Baumann, *Alexander's Great March.*
Pierre Grimal, *Stories of Alexander the Great.*

60

Suggested Activities

Naomi Mitchison, *Alexander the Great*, Then and There series.

Naomi Mitchison, *The Young Alexander the Great*.

L. Du Garde Peach, *Alexander the Great*, Ladybird book.

C. Mercer, *Alexander the Great*, Cassel Caravel series.

4 Hannibal: Enemy of Rome

Although Alexander's empire fell apart after his death the civilization of the Greeks endured over many of the lands which he had conquered. Greek was the common language of the Near East for centuries after Alexander's death: hence the New Testament was originally written in Greek.

New empires rose to compete for supremacy in the Mediterranean World—among them, Rome and Carthage.

Carthage was the great trading nation of the Western Mediterranean founded by the Phoenicians[1] in North Africa. Rome was founded in 753 B.C. according to legend and after centuries of warfare gained control over Italy. Then the first Punic War (Punic means Carthaginian) broke out between Rome and Carthage in which they fought for control over Sicily, the island between their empires. After a long and bitter struggle from 264–241 B.C. Rome won the war and Sicily became the first Roman province. This was the start of Rome's overseas empire.

Carthage then turned to Spain to extend her empire under the leadership of Hamilcar who was so determined to take revenge on Rome that he made his son Hannibal when only a child swear undying hatred to the Romans. When he was twenty-five Hannibal took over the Carthaginian army, picked a quarrel with Rome and decided to take her completely by surprise by marching his army over the Alps into Italy late in the year. He took with him another unwelcome surprise for the Romans— elephants.

The elephants were to cause Hannibal difficulties too. After crossing the Pyrenees in 218 B.C. he came to the river Rhône. As so often, Hannibal found an ingenious way of overcoming a difficulty.

[1] The Phoenicians came from the area around Tyre (see p. 44) and invented our alphabet.

62

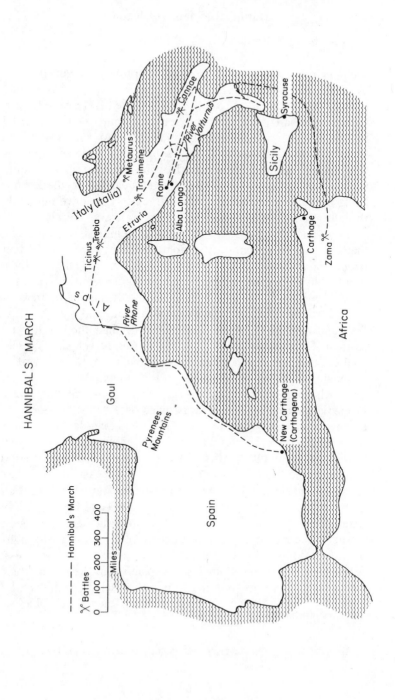

HANNIBAL'S MARCH

Italy (Italia)

Cannae

River Volturnus

Metaurus

Trasimene

Ticinus
Trebia

Rome

Etruria

Alba Longa

Sicily

Syracuse

River Rhone

Carthage

Zama

Africa

Gaul

Pyrenees Mountains

New Carthage (Carthagena)

Spain

– – – Hannibal's March
✕ Battles
Miles
0   100 200 300 400

Elephants Afloat

Various methods were, I believe, employed to get the elephants across; at any rate there are differing accounts of how it was done. According to one account, the beasts were herded close to the bank, and a notably ferocious one was then goaded by his driver, who promptly plunged into the water; the furious animal pursued him as he swam for his life and so drew the rest of the herd after him. Despite their terror at finding themselves in deep water, they were all carried to the farther bank by the sheer force of the current. It is more generally thought that they were ferried across on rafts—surely a safer method, and also, to judge by the result, a more likely one. The method was to prepare a big float, 200 feet long and 50 feet wide, which was held in position against the current by a number of strong cables led to the bank upstream; it was then covered with soil like a bridge, to induce the elephants to walk on to it without fear, as if they were still on land. To this float a second raft, of the same width but only half the length, and suitable for towing across the river, was attached. The elephants, the females leading, were driven on to the float— supposing it to be a solid road—and then passed on to the raft, when the ropes which lightly attached it to the float were immediately cast off, and it was towed over to the farther bank by rowing-boats. When the first batch had been landed, others were fetched and brought over. None of the animals showed any alarm so long as they were on what seemed the solid bridge: panic began only when the raft was cast off and they found themselves being carried into deep water; it was then that they showed fright, those nearest the edge backing away from the water and causing much jostling and confusion amongst their companions, until their very terror, at the sight of water all around them, seemed to freeze them into stillness. A few completely lost their heads and fell into the water; their riders were flung off, but the beasts themselves, stabilized by their weight, struggled on bit by bit till they found shallow water, and so got ashore.

Hannibal pressed on with all speed through the tribes of Gaul up towards the summit of the Alps.

Crossing the Alps

It is now October, and near the setting of the Pleiades. Nearly five months have passed since Hannibal and his original 102,000 set out from Carthagena. Apart from a few plundering attacks by small bands which are easily repulsed, the Gauls leave the Carthaginians alone. Now the enemy is nature herself. As the army climbs towards the frontier ridge the

MONTE VISO FROM THE VALLE PO
This may have been the pass used by Hannibal.

65

HANNIBAL IN THE ALPS

landscape becomes increasingly grim, bleak and hostile. First to disappear are the valley pastures and the homes of men; the tall pines overshadow the army for several miles, and then they, too, become thinner and sparser and finally fall away behind. Now there is nothing but bare rock and scrub, and the track winding endlessly up towards the snows. A piercing wind screams and whistles among the crags. During the night halts the resinous smell of pine wood fires blows across the camp; the rocks are ruddy with the flames, against which the little dark men from Africa and Spain huddle for protection against the unaccustomed cold. But fuel is scarce and has to be strictly conserved. Many of the troops, especially those weakened by wounds, fall victims of disease, and every morning, as the army strikes camp, it leaves behind sick men who can march no farther.

Maharbal is worried about fodder for the animals, especially for the elephants, for there is little among those lifeless rocks which yields even the scantiest food, and much of the carried fodder has been lost with the pack animals. The men might be sustained in an emergency by the flesh of such animals as are unfit for further work, but the elephants are not flesh-eaters, being accustomed to live on bark, leaves, roots and fruit. The great animals suffer severely, and some, worn out by hunger and the fatigue of that terrible climb, sink to their knees and die. Their flesh is cut up and eaten by the troops, and the carcases left to the vultures.

On the ninth day from the start of the climb a faint sound of cheering drifts down from the heights. The Carthaginian army, now reduced to about 35,000 men, drags for miles along a track, so narrow and tortuous that a man can see only a few hundred of his comrades ahead and behind. The rest are hidden behind the rocky flanks of the mountains, but the cheering continues, sometimes heard clearly, at other times blown away by the gale. It can have only one meaning. The vanguard must have reached the top of the pass, and, as the news is carried for mile after mile along the toiling ranks, men who seem to have reached the limit of exhaustion suddenly take fresh heart.

Staggering, stumbling, starving, blind and dizzy with fatigue, still they struggle on, up to the place where the last winter's snow, which had been creeping nearer and nearer down the slopes, covers the ground before them. They clamber on over the frozen ground, slipping, falling, rising and climbing on all fours. Rounding a rocky bluff they are met by a flurry of new snow, and for a time the peaks are lost in a storm of white flakes which, falling on the frozen snow of the previous winter, creates a new hazard. The skinny horses slip and slide, striving for a foothold, and many fall, but the great weight of the elephants now gives them an advantage, as their feet pound the new-fallen snow into a compact mass. The cheering grows louder, and each man, as he struggles over the lip of the pass, sees what he had never hoped to see. *The road climbs no higher.*

Along the narrow ridge, surrounded by mountains, thousands of men are huddled, black against the snow. Many lie exhausted; others, spurred on by their officers, are lighting fires and making camp, and as more and more men breast the ridge and join their companions the air is full of hoarse, exultant voices, some shouting, some sobbing with joy, while others gather on a rocky platform from which they can see the track winding steeply downwards to where the pines begin again, and a river gleams. Among that group is Hannibal and certain of his officers. Wrapped in their cloaks, they watch silently, their faces strained with the agony of the long march. Beside them the Gaulish guides, who have accompanied them all the way from the Rhône, are chattering and pointing. But Hannibal, Maharbal, Gisgo and the rest say little.

The snowstorm has blown away, and the sun, sinking behind the mountains which the army has climbed, lays a swathe of golden light across the green plain eight thousand feet below. More and more men press forward and gather around Hannibal. Their dark faces are emaciated and their eyes have a mad glint. The skins of many are festered with sores —the result of starvation and disease—and their stench is nauseating, even in that wild and windy place. In that hour, all share something of the exultation of their leader, the sense of triumph which comes to men who have endured the ultimate in pain and fatigue and yet have survived, while others have perished. They cannot understand the gibberish which the Gauls are pouring into the ears of their General, but one word, clumsily pronounced in a dozen different accents, spreads through the army. It is 'Italia'. After five months of marching, fighting, enduring, the Carthaginians look down, at last, on the land of the Romans.

The descent, far from being 'smooth', was in fact considerably worse than the climb, because the Italian side of the pass is even steeper than the French side, and the road was narrow, slippery and precipitous. 'Neither those who made the least stumble could prevent themselves from falling, nor, when fallen, remain in the same place, but rolled, men and beasts of burden, one upon another. They came to a rock much more narrow and formed of such perpendicular ledges, that a light-armed soldier, carefully making the attempt, and clinging with his hands to the bushes and roots around, could with difficulty lower himself down. The ground, even before very steep by nature, had been broken by a recent falling away of the earth into a precipice of nearly a thousand feet in depth. Here when the cavalry had halted, as if at the end of the journey, it was announced to Hannibal, wondering what obstructed the march, that the rock was impassable.'[1]

It is a dramatic moment, even in cold print, but much more so when one has seen the type of obstruction which, detached from its parent rock, pitches down the mountain side and falls thunderously into the valley below.

For hours the army has been making its slow, painful way down the mountain track. Then comes a halt and for several miles the army is stationary, unable to move. Hannibal and his officers struggle through the immobile mass, seeking to find the cause of the delay. Eventually they find it.

Blocking the narrowest part of the track, between the mountain wall and a 1,000-foot precipice, a huge rock bigger than a large house prevents further progress. It towers above the heads of the horses who stand idle, while their riders look at the seemingly impassable obstacle with despair on their faces. Some of the more agile troops have climbed the rock, using hand-holds, and are able to see over the top, but they report there are more and even larger rocks still blocking the road beyond. Light-armed troops could scale these obstacles, but the horsemen, pack animals and elephants are helpless. The

[1] These are the words of the Roman historian, Livy.

Carthaginians seem, as Livy says, 'to have reached the end of the journey'.

At first Hannibal tries to lead his army round the rock, over the pathless and untrodden regions around. But this proves impracticable, and finally he has to admit that the only solution is to destroy it. But how?

They have now reached somewhat lower ground where a few trees grew. Hannibal gives orders to his engineers to fell a considerable number of pines and make a huge pile of timber around the rock. As soon as a wind rises and begins to blow through the valley, the order is given to light the wood. When night falls the scene is an inferno. For hundreds of feet up the slopes the snow-covered rocks glow crimson as the flames leap high around the rock, and as more and more logs are thrown on to the fire, the great mass begins to glow a dull red. More and more fuel is flung on to the fire, while Hannibal, who is well-grounded in Greek science, watches and waits for the decisive moment. He has given orders to some of the foot soldiers to bring vinegar[1] in as large a quantity as possible. Now there are hundreds of these men, each with his vinegar-filled wineskin, silhouetted against the glow, waiting for a signal, while other men stand nearby, armed with heavy iron hammers and picks.

Suddenly Hannibal gives the order. The men rush through the smoke and, at the word of command, fling the liquid over the glowing mass. Relay after relay springs forward and as each contingent flings his burden into the flames, a deafening hiss rises and is echoed by the watching mountains. Clouds of blinding steam billow up from the rock and, through the cloud, the shapes of the hammer-and-pick-men are seen advancing, swinging their iron tools above their heads. Above the roar of the flames and the hiss of steam the sound of the hammers is like the clangour of Vulcan's smithy. As blow after blow rains on the tortured rocks the Carthaginians, half-mad with excitement, shout encouragement.

The rock splits and crumbles. Almost before the shattered

[1] Vinegar, which contains between three to nine per cent of acetic acid, was in Hannibal's time 'wine vinegar', i.e. wine of low alcoholic strength, produced by leaving wine exposed to the air. Hannibal's vinegar was probably just bad wine.

lumps are cool enough to grasp, men are dragging them away
and hurling them down the valley-side. Hannibal turns, halts
the hammer-men and gives orders to throw more fuel on the
flames. So the process is repeated, hour after hour, through
day and night, and as some men fall exhausted, others take
their place. Within four days the seemingly impassable
obstacle has disappeared, and Hannibal, besides having solved
an immediate, practical problem, enjoys the prestige of having
performed a feat, which, to most of his ignorant followers,
must have seemed magical.

*When he reached the Italian plains, Hannibal quickly
defeated the Romans twice, once at the river Ticinus and again
at the river Trebia, where the Roman general Sempronius attacked but found himself surrounded by a force of Carthaginians
hidden in the rushes by the river. After this the Romans were
more cautious and one of the Roman consuls,[1] Flaminius,
shadowed Hannibal without offering battle as he marched on
Rome. When Hannibal reached Lake Trasimene he noticed that
the ground was ideal for ambush. What happened next is told in
a story by the driver of Suru, the only one of Hannibal's
elephants which survived the crossing of the Alps.*

Lake Trasimene

The Cortonian Mountains come down so close to the edge of
Lake Trasimene that there is only a narrow passage-way from
the north to the south. On the road that runs along the shore
of the lake there is room for an army to march but not to be
drawn up in battle order. A broad belt of reeds, rooted in
marshy soil, surrounds the lake. Farther out it becomes deeper.
The Cortonian Mountains do not rise up steeply, but if the
heights are occupied an escape over them is as good as impossible.

Hannibal linked height to height with chains of slingers and
other lightly armed troops. He posted his most tried and
trusty mercenaries and horse troops in the ravines. Numidians

[1] Two consuls were elected each year at Rome. They were the most
important officials at Rome and commanded the army between them.

71

on fast horses were holding themselves in readiness to bar the defile at both ends. By the time that day dawned the trap was set for the Romans. The lake made its contribution: it covered the strip of shore with thick fog and turned the ravines into pools of mist. Only the heights were clear.

BATTLE OF LAKE TRASIMENE

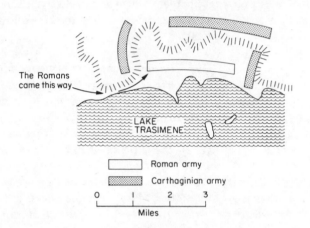

At sunrise the mist began to gleam with a blood-red light. Hannibal, sitting behind me on Suru, looked down at the trap with a satisfied air.

'No one will escape out of it,' he said. A dark fire was glowing in his eye. 'The mist is taking half our work away from us.'

I asked whether Suru would be in the battle.

'Are you afraid for him?' Hannibal tapped me on the shoulder comfortingly. 'He won't come to any harm—you've seen that for yourself. No one can touch him.'

It was quiet by the lake and on the mountain-tops. Everything depended on the enemy falling into the trap without his suspicion being aroused. No tell-tale sounds must come from the ambush which stretched along the lakeside. The mercenaries and horsemen knew this and lay on the watch without so much as whispering to one another.

Larks rose up out of the mist and hung lost in the blue, but they soon fell down again into their great white nest.

Then came the clatter of horses' hoofs. The Carthaginian rear-guard, who had been in charge of the camp-fires, withdrew hastily into the narrow defile. Their orders were to keep in contact with the enemy without engaging them in battle. Only farther south, on the open ground where Maharbal was waiting with his horse troops, were they to bring the enemy to a stand and cut off their escape out of the defile.

The clatter grew louder. Roman horse troops were on the heels of the rear-guard. Now they were joined by foot soldiers. It was a march of noisy phantoms as the Romans tried to find their way under the blanket of mist.

'It couldn't be better,' said Hannibal to Mago and Monomach and the other officers who had collected round him to receive their orders for the attack and to carry them back to their troops.

One of the officers from the rear-guard emerged from the mist and came riding up the hill as fast as his horse would carry him. He reported that the Romans had broken into the camp at early dawn. Astonished at finding it deserted, they had scattered the fires and then immediately set out in pursuit.

'Their ardour has not yet diminished,' Hannibal said mockingly, pointing down to the mist out of which the noise of marching legions rose. As the tramping of the vanguard revealed, their front ranks were already more than half-way through the defile. 'They can take their time,' remarked Hannibal. 'They have the longest day of the year before them —and so have we.' He sent the officers back to their troops, keeping a detachment of Berserkers and thirty horsemen with himself. The Berserkers were to clash their weapons together and roar as they alone could roar, when the time came to give the Carthaginians the signal to fall upon the Romans.

The mist was beginning to disperse. In some places the pools of mist lifted and helmets and armour caught the light. The Romans were advancing without any suspicion.

Now a horseman arrived from the north end of the defile. He reported that the last of the legionaries had moved in. Hannibal raised his arm. The Berserkers roared and made such a crashing noise with their weapons that Suru's ears rose up and he lifted his trunk in displeasure. I was able to quieten him, as the Berserkers were already charging down the hill and

73

the mist was swallowing them up. Now the sound of battle was coming from all along the lake. In echelon formation the Carthaginians pressed down on to the Romans, who now realized with horror that they were encircled.

The mist was dispersing quickly. Hannibal on Suru's back was on the look-out as if from a tower. Now what was happening down by the lake took on clear outlines. Some of the Romans were defending themselves with grim determination, others were taking flight and dragging fighting cohorts along with them. Many were trying to find a way of escape for themselves. But the ravines and the heights were barred to them. Only the lake was open to them. Some of the most desperate tried to hide in the belt of reeds and sank in the swamp. Several jumped into the lake and began to swim but their armour pulled them down. After two hours of battle there were none left but isolated fugitives, running or riding for their lives. At one spot only a cohort was left, fighting in regular battle formation. It was still defending itself when the mist had dispersed. Hannibal told me to ride towards it.

'The Consul is there, fighting for his life,' he said. 'He mustn't be allowed to escape.'

Suddenly Suru stood still and threw his trunk into the air and the horses of Hannibal's mounted escort tried to bolt.

'What was that?' Hannibal asked his horsemen.

'It was an earthquake!' some of them shouted back to him.

'The terror of the Romans has infected the earth,' said Hannibal mockingly.

'It was a real earthquake,' the horsemen maintained, and one of them pointed to the lake. Big waves were coming in although there was a complete calm.

'An earthquake, you're right,' said Hannibal in a voice that all could hear. 'Italy is trembling before us. Let us hope that it doesn't break into pieces.'

He ordered Suru and his escort to move on to the hill immediately above the fighting cohort. It was now completely surrounded. More and more Carthaginians were thrusting on to it. Along the lake there were countless rows of dead, chiefly Romans. There were still plenty of Carthaginians looking out for the enemy.

'It's going according to the plan,' I heard the man say who

was sitting behind me on Suru. From these words, and still more from the silence that followed them, I felt the tremendous willpower with which he had set the avalanche of destruction in motion and with which he had directed mercenaries, horses and their riders so that there was no way out for the Romans but death. And if anyone had told me at that moment that Hannibal had put the lake and the mountains where they were now, that he had arranged the belt of reeds, the ravines, and defiles so that they would serve for an ambush, that he had ordered the mist to rise and the earth to quake—I would have believed it. The mist had lain there just as long as was necessary to keep the trap hidden; it had lifted to show the Romans that there was no escape for them. Everything had helped to make Hannibal's victory complete.

The one cohort that was still fighting was dwindling away. Finally a detachment of Berserkers, in wedge formation, fought their way into it and up to the Consul. Flaminius fell, mortally wounded by a spear. The survivors now tried to fight their way out.

'Strike them down!' Hannibal yelled.

Never before had I heard a human being yell like that. It was the cry of a beast of prey, about to spring for a kill.

Hannibal urged the horsemen to pursue a small group of Romans who had fought their way out. 'Don't let any escape!'

Then ten or twelve Romans appeared from the other side, as if Hannibal's terrible cry had drawn them to him. Their weapons were covered with blood. It was a lost troop, and they were not looking for a way of escape but rather for a desperate action. They rushed at Hannibal. The legionaries had recognized him. That man in the red cloak, riding on the only elephant there was in the whole country, could be no one but Hannibal. They were breathless with running and their faces were distorted with hatred.

'Come to your death!' Hannibal shouted. He pulled his short sword out of its scabbard. I held the shield so that it protected both him and me in front.

When Suru saw the Romans he growled angrily. As this didn't bring them to a halt he began to attack them. Hannibal shouted again and Suru fell into a frenzy. The Romans surrounded him. He trampled two of them down and dealt a deadly blow with his trunk to two others. He struck the spear out of another's hand, seized him, and flung him into the air. He roared, and now Carthaginians came to our help from all sides, on foot and on horseback. The Romans who were still alive flung their spears at Hannibal. He beat off spear after spear with his sword. Now the Romans were surrounded, and they flung their swords at Hannibal in the hope of hitting him. He laughed and beat off sword after sword. He fought as one whom nothing can touch. He only missed one sword. It struck my right arm and tore it open from the shoulder to the elbow.

A few minutes later the Romans were all cut down. Until the last their eyes had been fixed on Hannibal and they had cursed him.

'They got you,' I heard Hannibal say. 'We'll soon have you bandaged up. Make Suru kneel down!'

Suru knelt down without waiting for the order from me.

'I've never had a better elephant,' said Hannibal, dismounting, 'and never a better driver.' He examined my wound. 'No one of your mettle would die of that,' he said.

Suru didn't stand up again, as he otherwise always did when he was rid of his load.

'He's killed five,' Hannibal cried to the officers and mercenaries. 'Let him be an example to you!'

'Stand up, Suru,' I said coaxingly, while my wound was being bandaged. He made an effort to get up but fell back on to his knees.

'Stand up!' I said again. 'It's all over.'

'Stand up, old fellow!' Hannibal now joined in. 'You've saved my life and the little Carthaginian's. The war will soon be over—stand up!'

And now with a great effort Suru did stand up. Then I saw streaks of blood on the grey pillars that supported him. On his neck and on his shoulder there were gaping wounds the size of the palm of my hand.

'What have you been doing, old fellow?' asked Hannibal in alarm.

I tore myself away from the man who was bandaging me and took a few steps towards Suru. Then I fell flat on my face and knew no more.

76

Oxen on Fire

The Romans had learnt a lesson. They made Quintus Fabius Maximus[1] dictator in charge of the army and he decided to adopt new tactics: to shadow Hannibal, cut off his supplies and try to trap him, without engaging their whole army in battle. It soon seemed as if the new plan had succeeded.

Oxen on Fire

Firmly pursuing his strategy of containment, Fabius garrisoned Casilinum in the enemy's rear. The river Volturnus

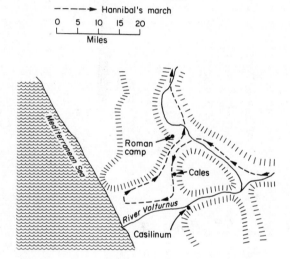

HANNIBAL TRICKS FABIUS

from Casilinum to the sea prevented any retreat southward, and the colony of Cales barred the outlet from the plain. Between Casilinum and Cales the hills formed an unbroken barrier, steep and wooded, with only a few paths already secured by Roman soldiers.

Fabius had acted very cleverly. By all the rules of orthodox warfare, Hannibal was caught in a trap. He could not expect to winter in Campania, since once it had exhausted its supplies

[1] Maximus means 'Greatest'. Later the name Cunctator ('Delayer') was added because of his tactics.

his army could not stay where it was, without a single town in its possession, and with no means of pasturing its cattle and storing the masses of plunder which it had accumulated. Besides many thousands of cattle, Hannibal was encumbered with numerous prisoners, besides corn, oil, wine and other provisions. The only road along which his army could escape was that along which it came. This narrow mountain pass was guarded by a strong detachment of Roman soldiers while Fabius, with the main army, was camped at some distance away, watching the pass. . . .

It is the third watch on a calm summer night in 217 B.C. Throughout the day there has been no unusual activity in the Carthaginian camp. Apart from the sentries and the men guarding the pass, most of the Roman army is sleeping. An orderly enters the tent of Fabius and wakes the dictator. As he rubs the sleep from his eyes and looks about him, he hears, in the far distance, the excited shouts of men. Is the camp being attacked? No, the sound is too far away for that. Throwing on his clothes, Fabius leaves the tent and finds Marcus Minucius, his Master of Horse, gathered with other officers outside. They are all looking, not at the pass along which they expected Hannibal to attempt his escape, but at the hillsides above it.

The sight is enough to alarm and astonish them. Up the steep, dark slopes thousands of lights are moving, dipping and swaying, but all moving towards the heights. Some of the pin-points of light are already nearing the crest of the ridge while below other flames, as if of torches, are massed in a glittering constellation, moving haphazardly, now right, now left, then up, as if carried by men seeking a way of escape from the blocked pass and over the hills.

'We've got them, Sir!' shouts the excited Minucius. 'The fool thinks he can get away over the hills at night, while we're asleep! But only a few have got away. Move the army down to the foot of the pass *now*, and we can stop the rest!' He implores Fabius to give the order, but the dictator remembers Sempronius at Trebia, and Flaminius at Lake Trasimene. 'No,' he says gravely. 'This is another Punic trick. We have a force guarding the pass. They'll deal with these men. *The army will not move. We shall stay here until dawn. Don't move. I forbid you.*' In vain Minucius and the other officers try to persuade

Fabius to attack, while more and more glittering lights move up the dark hillside and over the crest.

Meanwhile, the Romans guarding the pass, seeing the lights and believing that the enemy are trying to outwit them, leave their posts and scramble up the hillside. It is hard going in the dark, for the mountainsides are steep and treacherous, and it is some time before the more agile soldiers come close enough to get to grips with their adversaries. A young centurion, sword in hand, runs towards one of the moving lights and then stops, bewildered. His companions, when they join him on the heights, look on in astonishment and disappointment before slowly they sheathe their swords. What they see before them is a huddle of cattle with burning brands tied to their horns. From above and below they hear the excited cries of their comrades who, like them, are climbing the heights in pursuit of imaginary enemies.

The cries change to shouts of disgust and anger. Realizing that they have been tricked, they begin to hurry down the hillside again, back to the posts they have deserted. Then they get another surprise. They blunder into dark shapes standing among the rocks, the shapes not of cattle but of men. Quietly, but with deadly efficiency, the small force of picked Carthaginian troops who have driven the cattle up the slopes, fall on the dismayed Romans and cut them down. No one knows whether the shadows around him conceal men or beasts. Leaderless, out of their accustomed formation, alarmed and terrified by the darkness and the uncertainty, the Romans wait for the dawn.

Hannibal is now down in the unguarded pass far below, joking with Maharbal, Hasdrubal and the rest, as they move unmolested over the mountains to safety. Behind them march the thousands of Africans, Numidians, Gauls, loaded with the plunder of Campania, and driving before them some 2,000 cattle. Before dawn they will be out of danger and on their way to the lush grasslands of Apulia, to which their commander has promised to lead them.

When the dawn light seeps across the green Campanian plain, it reveals the Roman army still within its camp, where Fabius is still assuring his officers that this is yet another Punic trick. He is right, of course, but this time the victim is

Fabius. When his scouts, whom he has sent to reconnoitre the Carthaginian camp, return, it is with despair and frustration on their faces. Hannibal has gone; and so has all his army with its booty.

Once again Hannibal had studied the mind of his opponent and taken his measure. Both Sempronius and Flaminius were rash fools who fell into the traps prepared for them, but Fabius was not a fool, and Hannibal knew this. If 'the Delayer' had been as impetuous as either of the two Consuls whom Hannibal had already defeated, he would have been deceived, and would have led his army out of the camp in time to intercept Hannibal's main force. Being a cautious and prudent general, he stayed where he was and so allowed the Carthaginians to get away.

However, the Romans grew tired of shadowing Hannibal, dismissed Fabius and appointed two consuls with orders to bring Hannibal to battle. They attacked Hannibal at Cannae but were themselves killed together with nearly the whole of their two armies. The Romans never attacked Hannibal again in pitched battle in Italy. Instead they decided to wear him down by adopting delaying tactics again and putting Quintus Fabius Maximus in charge of the army.

It took twelve years to starve Hannibal out of Italy. At one time Hasdrubal, Hannibal's brother, led a relief force over the Alps but was killed at the battle of the River Metaurus in 207 B.C. before he could join up with Hannibal.

Meanwhile the Romans had discovered a brilliant general, Scipio, who had grown up during the war and learnt much from studying Hannibal's tactics. When Hannibal returned to Carthage, Scipio followed him. In the final battle of the war at Zama in 202 B.C. Scipio defeated Hannibal and Carthage surrendered.

The Romans forced the Carthaginians to give up all their empire. Rome was now the leading state in the western Mediterranean area. Soon she became involved in further wars with states in the East; Greece and Macedon became Roman provinces. Greece was conquered by the Romans because the Greek cities never joined together as one country and so could not resist the attack of a large united foreign invader. Rome took control of Greece, but the civilization of Greece took control of Rome and the Romans' way of life was completely changed. Carthage was destroyed in 146 B.C. when Rome picked a quarrel with Carthage and razed the city to the ground. By that time most of Spain too had been conquered and Rome was without doubt the major power in the Mediterranean world—a position she was to hold for over 500 years.

Suggested Activities

Writing

1. Imagine you were an elephant driver helping to get the elephants across the river Rhône. Describe what happened.

2. Suppose you were a Roman meeting an elephant for the first time or a Carthaginian meeting snow for the first time. Write home telling your family what you saw and felt.

3. Write a few days in the diary of Hannibal or one of his soldiers.

4. Describe the battle of Lake Trasimene as if you were a Roman soldier who escaped.

Drawing

1. Draw a map or diagram with measurements of how the elephants crossed the river Rhône. Use the description on p. 64 which will tell you what you need.

2. Draw a picture of the elephants crossing the river Rhône.

3. Draw a map of Hannibal's march (see p. 63).

4. Draw a series of pictures or a strip cartoon to tell the story of Hannibal's life.

Acting

1. Interview Hannibal as if for radio or television after the battle of Lake Trasimene. You could ask the following questions.

(a) Congratulations on your victory . . . but some people do say that you won the battle by a trick. What do you think?

(b) Do you think the Romans will ever dare come out again to fight you?

(c) You haven't been able to bring any siege weapons with you, so do you think you will be able to capture Rome?

(d) Do you think Rome's allies will join you now to be on the winning side?

(e) You obviously hate the Romans. When did this hatred start?

(f) When you came to the river Rhône did you think at first that you would be able to get the elephants across?

(g) Weren't you taking a great risk trying to cross the Alps so late in the year?

(h) What have you been proudest of doing so far? Would you tell us again of how you did it?

(i) How long do you think the war will last?

(j) Some people say that you are the greatest general there has been—even greater than Alexander. What do you think?

2. Suppose that Alexander and Hannibal met in the Underworld. Act out the conversation they had each arguing that he was the better general.

3. Act the scene in the Roman camp when news is brought about Hannibal's oxen on the hillside.

Finding Out

1. Aeneas was a Trojan warrior who escaped from Troy when it was captured by the Greeks, made his way to Italy and was the ancestor of Romulus and Remus (see the next suggested activity). Find out about some of the adventures Aeneas had and in particular about his meeting with Dido who according to legend founded Carthage (see suggested activity No 5 below). Read K. McLeish, *Land of the Eagles* or *The Story of Aeneas*, and R. B. Taylor, *The Aeneid of Virgil*.

2. Find out the story of Romulus and Remus and how according to legend Rome was founded.

3. Find out more about the Etruscans.

4. Rome was 20 miles from the sea on the river Tiber where it was crossed by roads in the centre of Italy. Do you think

this helped Rome to be powerful and prosperous? Draw a map to show this.

5. Find out more about Carthage and the Phoenicians.

6. Find out more about the Punic Wars, in particular the Second Punic War when Hannibal attacked Rome. Draw diagrams of the main battles. See p. 72, and find out more about the battles of Cannae, Metaurus and Zama (see J. Defrasne, *Stories of Ancient Rome*).

Further Reading

Hans Baumann, *I Marched with Hannibal*.
J. Defrasne, *Stories of Ancient Rome*.
H. E. L. Mellersh, *Carthage*, Young Historian series.
R. M. Ogilvie, *Stories from Livy*.
E. Royston Pike, *Finding out about the Etruscans*.
D. Phillips Birt, *Finding out about the Phoenicians*.

5 Caesar and the Roman Conquest of Britain

When Julius Caesar was forty his friends found him one day in despair. 'Alexander,' he said, 'had conquered the world long before my age while I so far have achieved nothing worthy of myself.' Yet Caesar became so famous that for over 2,000 years after his death kings have been called by his name.[1]

Two years later came the turning point in Caesar's career. He became consul and was put in charge of an army with which he invaded Gaul (now France) and over a period of ten years conquered it. While he was in Gaul, in 55 B.C., Caesar decided

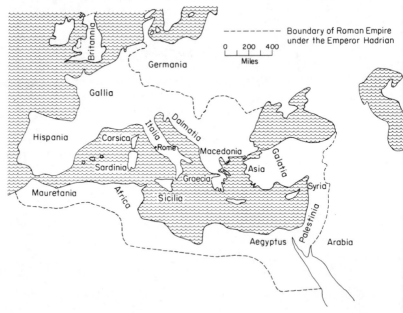

THE ROMAN EMPIRE
Which modern countries have names like the Roman ones ?

------- Boundary of Roman Empire
under the Emperor Hadrian

0   200   400
Miles

Britannia
Germania
Gallia
Hispania
Corsica
Italia
Dalmatia
Rome
Macedonia
Galatia
Asia
Sardinia
Graecia
Syria
Mauretania
Africa
Sicilia
Palestinia
Aegyptus
Arabia

---

[1] The Roman Emperors were called Caesar until the fifth century, the Russian emperors Tsar until 1917. The Shah of Persia is still called by his name.

to invade Britain. He was attracted by reports of the great wealth of the island.

Caesar's Raid

At about 9 am on an autumn morning, over 2,000 years ago, eighty ships appeared off the cliffs of Dover. On the clifftops thousands of charioteers, horsemen and spearmen, looked

JULIUS CAESAR

85

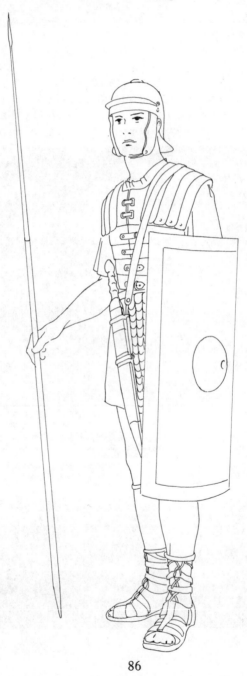

down on the Roman fleet as it rolled and pitched in the Channel swell.

'I saw the enemy forces standing under arms along the heights,' writes Caesar. 'At this point of the coast precipitous cliffs tower above the water, making it possible to fire directly on to the beaches. It was clearly no place to attempt a landing, so we rode at anchor until 3.30 pm awaiting the rest of the fleet. I summoned my staff and company commanders (centurions), passed on to them the information obtained by Volusenus, and explained my plans. They were warned that, as tactical demands, particularly at sea, are always uncertain and subject to rapid change, they must be ready to act at a moment's notice on the briefest order from myself. The meeting then broke up; both wind and tide were favourable, the signal was given to weigh anchor, and after moving about eight miles up channel the ships were grounded on an open and evenly shelving beach.'

Thus speaks the dry voice of the commanding officer, appraising the situation, making decisions, giving orders. But how did the landing appear to the other thousands taking part—the legionaries crammed in the rolling hulks, with the cold sea spray dashing on their helmets, men from Italy and Gaul who had marched two thousand miles behind their brilliant commander, land-soldiers hardened by a score of campaigns, but unaccustomed to the sea, and fearful, perhaps, of what lay beyond the white cliffs which towered above their little ships? Caesar had led them out of many tight spots, often 'snatching victory from the jaws of defeat'. But had he gone a little too far this time?

THE ROMAN LEGIONARY (*left*)

For attack the legionary carried two javelins and a sword. He would first advance within range of the enemy and throw his javelins, which had a wooden handle and a soft metal shaft leading to a hard head. If the javelin missed its mark, the soft metal would bend and the enemy would be unable to use it, or if it stuck in a shield it would be difficult to remove and weigh the shield down. The legionary would then close in while the enemy were still disorganized by the javelin attack and stab at his opponent's body with his sword.

For defence the legionary was well protected, as you can see. Underneath his armour he wore a tunic stretching to the knees, a woollen cloak and a scarf to prevent the metal of the armour chafing his neck.

And the Britons on the clifftops, wheeling their horses and chariots and, under the shouted orders of their commanders moving steadily westward, keeping watchful eyes on that flotilla as it coasted towards Walmer, seeking a landing place. What was in their minds? Some of them knew the Romans, had fought them in Gaul; they were familiar with those indomitable phalanxes of armed men who stood unmoved against the rushing chariots, hurling their deadly throwing-spears which stuck in one's shield and then bent at the head, so that one had to throw away the useless shield and rely on the sword; that slashing-sword which the Romans despised, trained as they were to kill with the thrusting-point. The Romans were men, like themselves, but a different kind of men; all dressed and armed alike, and moving in disciplined formations, as if 1,000 bodies were impelled by only one brain.

When they advanced, with shields interlocked above their heads, it was as if one was fighting, not beings of flesh and blood, but some metal monster without a soul. One had seen them marching through the passes of the Ardennes with their baggage-trains, wagons, tents and equipment, moving and halting at the word of command, building their fortified camps at night, camps which were like small cities, with earthworks surrounding neat, tented enclosures. One fought them, and was defeated. They moved on to the banks of the Seine, the Meuse and the Sambre, where one's fathers had lived. And after they had moved on, there followed, inevitably, the officials and tax gatherers. . . .

And now they are here, on the coast of Britain to which one had hoped they could not follow. The young men are confident as young men usually are, though among the older warriors there are some who doubt if the wild, undisciplined courage of the Celt can ever prevail against these men of steel. But now, from the vanguard of the British army comes a roar. The Romans have grounded their ships, and are coming ashore.

'On account of their large draught,' wrote Caesar, 'the ships could not be beached except in deep water; and the troops, besides being ignorant of the locality, had their hands full; weighted with a mass of heavy armour, they had to jump from their ships, stand firm in the surf, and fight at the same time. But the enemy knew their ground, they could hurl their weapons boldly from dry land or shallow water, and gallop their horses which were trained for this kind of work. Our men were terrified; they were inexperienced in this kind of fighting and lacked that dash and drive which always characterized their land battles.'

If only one had but one account by a Legionary of that moment! The shingle beach at Walmer, where the Romans landed, shelves steeply. The heavy wooden hulls dug their prows into the beach many yards from the shore. On the beach and behind it were the massed tribesmen, shouting and hurling their spears into the Roman ships, which canted over. The flap of sails mixed with orders, curses, words of command. A rain of spears fell among the packed troops. A man fell backwards on the deck, vomiting blood. Another pitched into the sea, a spear in his back. Confused cries from the other ships drifted down on the wind, mixed with the crash of breakers and the long-drawn hiss of the undertow. It was a moment of panic and uncertainty.

'Then', writes Caesar, 'the standard-bearer of the 10th Legion, calling on the Gods to bless the Legion through his act, shouted: "Come on, men! Jump, unless you want to betray your standard to the enemy! I, at any rate, shall do my duty to my country and my commander." He threw himself into the sea and started forward with the eagle. The rest were not going to disgrace themselves; cheering wildly they leaped down, and when the men in the next ships saw them they too quickly followed their example.'

At first the fight was bitter; the legionaries and their auxiliary troops, accustomed to fight in disciplined formations, were confused.

... our fellows were unable to keep their appointed standards, because men from different ships were falling in under the first one they reached, and a good deal of confusion resulted. The Britons, of course, knew all the shallows, standing on dry land, they watched the men disembark in small parties, galloped down, attacked them as they struggled through the surf, and surrounded them with superior numbers while others opened fire on the exposed flanks of the isolated units. I therefore had the warships' boats and scouting vessels filled with troops, so that help could be sent to any point where the men seemed to be in difficulties. When every one was ashore and formed up, the legions charged. . . .

This was the decisive moment. Once ashore, the Romans could fight as units under their commanders. The Britons retired in disorder, but Caesar was unable to follow up his advantage, since, as he tells us 'the cavalry transports had been unable to hold their course and make the island. That was the only thing that deprived us of a decisive victory.'

Caesar's aim in this expedition was to spy out the land and after a few days he returned to Gaul. He returned the following year but met with greater resistance than he had expected and the wealth of the island proved to be less than he had thought. Caesar made peace with the British chiefs and the Romans did not return for nearly a century.

When Caesar returned to Italy from Gaul civil war broke out between him and Pompey. Pompey was a very powerful Roman general whose troops were a danger to Caesar. After a series of whirlwind campaigns, Caesar won and became dictator of the whole Roman world. As dictator he made many enemies, men who resented the loss of freedom. Among them were Cassius and Brutus, a descendant of the Brutus who had driven an Etruscan king out of Rome centuries before. They formed a conspiracy to kill Caesar in the senate house. The day chosen was the Ides (15th) of March, 44 B.C.

The Ides of March

They say that strange signs were shown and strange apparitions were seen. As for the lights in the sky, the crashing sounds heard in all sorts of directions by night, the solitary specimens of birds coming down into the forum, all these, perhaps, are scarcely worth mentioning in connexion with so great an event as this. But the philosopher Strabo says that a great crowd of men all on fire were seen making a charge; also that from the hand of a soldier's slave a great flame sprang out so that the hand seemed to the spectators to be burning away; but when the flame died out, the man was uninjured. He also says that when Caesar himself was making a sacrifice, the heart of the animal being sacrificed was missing—a very bad omen indeed, since in the ordinary course of nature no animal can exist without a heart. There is plenty of authority too for the following story: a soothsayer warned Caesar to be on his guard against a great danger on the day of the month of March which the Romans call the Ides; and when this day had come, Caesar, on his way to the senate-house, met the soothsayer and greeted him jestingly with the words: 'Well, the Ides of March have come,' to which the soothsayer replied in a soft voice: 'Yes, but they have not yet gone.' And on the previous day Marcus Lepidus was entertaining Caesar at supper and Caesar, according to his usual practice, happened to be signing letters as he reclined at table. Meanwhile the conversation turned to the question of what sort of death was the best, and, before anyone else could express a view on the subject, Caesar cried out: 'The kind that comes unexpectedly.' After this, when he was sleeping as usual by the side of his wife, all the doors and windows of the bedroom flew open at once; Caesar, startled by the noise and by the light of the moon shining down on him, noticed that Calpurnia was fast asleep, but she was saying something in her sleep which he could not make out and was groaning in an inarticulate way. In fact she was dreaming at that time that she was holding his murdered body in her arms and was weeping over it. When it was day, she implored Caesar, if it was possible, not to go out and begged him to postpone the meeting of the senate. Caesar himself, it seems, was affected and by no means easy in his mind. And when the prophets, after making many sacrifices, told him that the omens were unfavourable, he decided to send for Antony and to dismiss the senate.

At this point Decimus Brutus, surnamed Albinus, intervened. Fearing that if Caesar escaped this day the whole plot would come to light, he spoke derisively of the prophets.

While he was speaking, Brutus took Caesar by the hand and began to lead him towards the door. And before he had gone far from the door a slave belonging to someone else tried to approach him, but being unable to get near him because of the crowds who pressed round him, forced his way into the house and put himself into the hands of Calpurnia, asking her to keep him safe until Caesar came back, since he had some very important information to give him.

Then there was Artemidorus, a Cnidian by birth, and a teacher of Greek philosophy who, for that reason, had become acquainted with Brutus and his friends. He had thus acquired a very full knowledge of the conspiracy and he came to Caesar with a small document in which he had written down the information which he intended to reveal to him. But when he saw that Caesar took each document that was given to him and then handed it to one of his attendants, he came close up to him and said: 'Read this one, Caesar, and read it quickly and by yourself. I assure you that it is important and that it concerns you personally.' Caesar then took the document and was several times on the point of reading it, but was prevented from doing so by the numbers of people who came to speak to him. It was the only document which he did keep with him and he was still holding it in his hand when he went on into the senate.

It may be said that all these things could have happened as it were by chance. But the place where the senate was meeting that day and which was to be the scene of the final struggle and of the assassination made it perfectly clear that some heavenly power was at work, guiding the action and directing that it should take place just here. For here stood a statue of Pompey, and the building had been erected and dedicated by Pompey as one of the extra amenities attached to his theatre. Indeed it is said that, just before the attack was made on him, Caesar turned his eyes towards the statue of Pompey and silently prayed for its goodwill.

Now Antony, who was a true friend of Caesar's and also a strong man physically, was detained outside the senate house by Brutus Albinus, who deliberately engaged him in a long conversation. Caesar himself went in and the senate rose in his honour. Some of Brutus' party took their places behind his chair and others went to meet him as though they wished to support the petition being made by Tillius Cimber on behalf of his brother who was in exile. So, all joining in with him in his entreaties, they accompanied Caesar to his chair. Caesar took his seat and continued to reject their request; as they pressed him more and more urgently, he began to grow angry with them. Tillius then took hold of his toga with both hands and pulled it down from his neck. This was the signal for the attack. The first blow was struck by Casca, who wounded Caesar in the neck with his dagger. The wound was not mortal and not even a deep one, coming as it did from a man who was no doubt much disturbed in mind at the beginning of such a daring venture. Caesar, therefore, was able to turn round and grasp the knife and hold on to it. At almost the same moment the striker of the blow and he who was struck cried out together—Caesar, in Latin, 'Casca, you villain, what are you doing?' while Casca called to his brother in Greek: 'Help, brother.'

So it began, and those who were not in the conspiracy were so horror-struck and amazed at what was being done that they were afraid to run away and afraid to come to Caesar's help; they were too afraid even to utter a word. But those who had come prepared for the murder all bared their daggers and hemmed Caesar in on every side. Whichever way he turned he met the blows of daggers and saw the cold steel aimed at his face and at his eyes. So he was driven this way and that, and like a wild beast in the toils, had to suffer from the hands of each one of them; for it had been agreed that they must all take part in this sacrifice and all flesh themselves with his blood. Because of this compact Brutus also gave him one wound in the groin. Some say that Caesar fought back against all the rest, darting this way and that to avoid the blows and crying out for help, but when he saw that Brutus had drawn his dagger, he covered his head with his toga and sank down to the ground. Either by chance or because he was pushed there by his murderers, he fell down against the pedestal on which the statue of Pompey stood, and the pedestal was drenched with his blood, so that one might have thought that Pompey himself was presiding over this act of vengeance against his enemy, who lay there at his feet struggling convulsively under so many wounds. He is said to have received twenty-three wounds. And many of his assailants were wounded by each other, as they tried to plant all those blows in one body.

So Caesar was done to death and, when it was over, Brutus stepped forward with the intention of making a speech to explain what had been done. The senators, however, would not wait to hear him. They rushed out through the doors of the building and fled to their homes.

The Roman people, roused by Mark Antony, Caesar's friend, drove Brutus and Cassius from Rome. They were later defeated in battle and killed by Caesar's successor, his great-nephew Augustus. Augustus and Antony then divided the Roman world between them but subsequently quarrelled and civil war broke out. Antony was helped by Cleopatra the queen of Egypt who was in love with him, but they were defeated and both committed suicide. Augustus became the first Roman emperor. He was the emperor Caesar Augustus who sent out a decree that a registration should be made throughout the Roman world when Jesus Christ was born.[1]

The Romans returned to Britain in A.D. *43 led by the emperor Claudius. Caratacus, King of the Trinobantes, called by the Britons Caradoc, gathered an army from many tribes to meet the Romans. In the story which follows two Celtic[2] boys, Gwydion and Math, with their dog Bel, go to see the battle.*

Ha! Among the Trumpets!

Under the summer sun that day the fate of a country was to be decided, and the two boys, watching from a hillock over half a mile away from the conflict, gazed with set faces, their hearts beating with excitement. Even Bel was caught up in this frenzied atmosphere and, as trumpets blew from the Roman side and the long war-horns howled from the Celtic side, the small hound leapt on his thong-lead with an excitement as pronounced as that of his young master, whining and scratching the springy turf, as he tried to break away and run from this immense turmoil which now seemed to approach and now retreat from the watchers on the hill. Down there it seemed that half the world had assembled to do battle, for the plain was now dark with a multitude of men.

The Roman cohorts were in position now, the sturdy, loud-

[1] St. Luke's gospel, chapter 2, verse 1.

[2] i.e. British. Celtic tribes had crossed over from the continent to settle in Britain from as early as 800 B.C.

Ha! Among the Trumpets!

ROMAN BRITAIN

Showing some of the main towns, roads and tribes

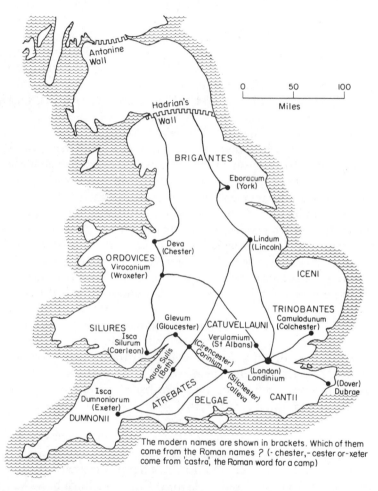

The modern names are shown in brackets. Which of them come from the Roman names ? (- chester, - cester or -xeter come from 'castra', the Roman word for a camp)

voiced centurions and decurions pushing and beating the headstrong legionaries into the formation they required; the noble young officers, with their red horse-hair plumes floating in the breeze and their blue cloaks puffing out behind them like smoke, galloping from company to company, calling out now and again, and pointing here and there with their gilded staffs or long cavalry swords.

The infantry of the Legion was in place, solid and waiting, each man bearing his shield well before his body, his long lance held up and slightly pointed forward, ready for the command to advance.

Then a great hush settled over the tumultuous preparations, for there was a series of blasts on the long silver trumpets, and line after line of Roman archers marched forward, past the waiting ranks of infantrymen, accompanied by cheers as they went, each man with his head held proudly and erect, to take up their positions at the very front of the foremost line, protected only by one rank of shieldmen.

Gwydion watched them in admiration, as did the various groups of Celtic tribesmen who sat, here and there, facing the Romans, on the broad plain. Gwydion looked over towards his own massed countrymen, and recognized many of the tribes by the colours of their tunics and plaids; Cantii, Trinobantes, his mother's own people, the Atrebates, even certain groups of Iceni, who had always spoken well of Rome in the past; but he noticed that there were no Brigantes, even though their old queen, Cartimandua, had been one of the first to promise help to Caratacus when his great father, Cunobelinus, had died a year or so before.

These tribes were all spearmen and swordmen and archers. The cavalry were out of sight, behind that high hill which lay over towards the city. So were the chariots, which would be led by the king himself. These would not go into action until the crowding, jostling footmen had had their opportunity of slaughter and plunder, for that was a standing agreement between the battle-leaders of various tribes.

Then, far from the rear of the Roman multitudes, came riding men in coloured skin tunics, and high sheepskin hats, each one with a feather, and usually a heron's feather, stuck in its point. Gwydion stared at them, at their long horn bows and little shaggy ponies, and he gasped. For now he knew what that man was whom he had seen in the wood that night—a Roman horseman, a wild rider from Scythia, and not a god at all! And as his mind went back, he wondered whether the man he had seen was a spy, or a deserter from Rome, a horseman who was tired of serving a heartless Empire that, at the end of his twenty years of service would offer him little more reward than mere citizenship of Rome. .... But Gwydion's thoughts were rudely shattered then, for, with a wild skirling of horns and beating of gongs, the Celts opened the attack, moving swiftly down the hill in small vicious groups, like a great cloud shadow on a sunlit day, harrying the enemy at various points and in various ways, some with the spear, some with bows and some with knives, at close quarters. Yet though the tribes always left heaps of dead, their own and those of Rome, behind them, the formation of the Legion did not falter, and the shield-wall stayed, as solid as before.

Here and there among the widespread tumult the boys saw the tribesmen tearing off their clothes and armour and, singing a wild death song, begin to dash across the stony plain towards the stolid ranks of Rome. Sometimes, as these madmen approached, their enemies cheered them on, and even laughed at them, until they fell, pierced by sword or javelin, a yard or two from the impregnable shield-wall.

This sporadic fighting might have gone on for long enough, with the archers and the shaggy horsemen waiting, smiling superciliously, and the great gold Eagle of the Legion still shining proudly in the afternoon sun; but then something else happened. Suddenly there was a shower of rain, which beat down out of the summer sky without warning, and in the midst of it appeared a great, brightly coloured rainbow that seemed to arch itself immediately over the Celtic tribes. A great whisper of wonder rose from the armies, a sound like the hissing waves of the sea on a rocky shore; and the massed tribesmen seemed to shudder as they drew back and fell to their knees, many of them, offering thanks to their gods for this omen of victory. Then the shower passed as suddenly as it had begun and the rainbow went with it, leaving the battlefield a place of great stillness and expectation.

Then, before the footmen of the tribes could regain their feet to attack again, there came the high wailing sound of the king's own war-horns, the signal for the chariots, and to the wonder of the boys, there rose above the hill the many-coloured pennants of these carts of death.

'Look, oh look!' said Gwydion aloud. 'The king has come! The king has come, and my father will be close to him in the battle line!'

Then, as the boy had said, foremost in the long line came the ebony and gold chariot of Caratacus, its red dragon flag furling and unfurling as the winds caught it and let it go again. At the king's right hand, and smiling at his master, stood Gwydion's father, Caswallawn, holding the reins lightly and waiting for the signal to charge. Gwydion stared at the family chariot, for it looked so different now, so dangerous and even wicked, though he had played on it, climbing in and out of it in the stables for as long as he could remember, and he had never thought of it as being a cruel weapon of destruction before. Now it thrilled him that his house should be so represented, and so near to the king too. He saw the golden-haired Caratacus, with his great horned golden helmet, turn and say something to his father, and the chariots manœuvred close together so that the two men could shake each other by the hand.

'Did you see that!' said Gwydion in an ecstasy. 'Oh, I wish I could be with them today! Don't you, Math?'

But Math stared, dark-eyed and serious, for he was watching another people, not his own, and he did not see the fine glory of it all as Gwydion did. He did not answer.

Then the king took the red dragon banner and took it in his hands and whirled it round his head, once, twice, and on the third sweep flung it high into the air. A gasp of wonder broke from the Roman ranks. Then down came the banner and Caratacus caught it and shouted. And from the throats of all the tribesmen came the great deep shout, 'Caradoc! Caradoc! We are your dogs, who wish to die for you! Caradoc! Caradoc!' Math had time merely to glance at his friend, and to note the tears of glory that stood in his light-blue eyes, and then the chariots began to roll forward, slowly at first, for the charioteers found it difficult to manage their restive horses who knew that they were in battle again after many months of idleness in field and barn.

Then, like some monster slowly gathering speed, the chariot line moved, first at a walk, then at a canter, and at last at a gallop; and from the massed cohorts came sharp orders and the sudden screams of the Roman trumpets. In his excitement, Gwydion moved from the shelter of the rock behind which he had been standing, and ran out into the open. Math followed him, himself almost caught up in the magic of the battle. Then came the clash, and for a while there was nothing but a vast maelstrom of shields and spears and charioteers tumbled in the dust.

Gwydion scanned the broken line and saw that his father and the king were safe. Then he looked at the Roman line, but all the spaces had been filled, and it was as though there had been no charge. The chariots retired for a while, drawing back a hundred paces, while the footmen went in again, hacking and stabbing and trying to break the first shield-wall. Then they too withdrew, leaving many of their comrades behind them, and once again the king waved his red banner; but this time, before the charge could roll forward on its way, a strange thing happened—the shield-wall seemed to melt away, the line of men swinging like a great gate, to right and to left, leaving exposed the archers, each one erect and bearing his bow drawn to its full and directed towards the Celts. There was a sudden call on the horn and a shout from a centurion who controlled the archers, and the air was full of the hum of arrows, as though a great beehive had suddenly been kicked over and the angry swarm had rushed out to avenge the outrage. Charioteers toppled from their platforms, axemen who stood on the central shaft between the horses fell, clutching their throats or their chests; horses snorted and sank to their knees. Then the shield -wall closed again and the archers were hidden.

'A Roman trick,' shouted Gwydion. 'The trick of a wicked people!' But Math did not know what to think; he clasped his friend's hand tightly, and looked to see that Caswallawn was still safe, still beside his king.

So the chariots moved again, those that were left, and once again the shield-wall took them, swaying a little, breaking here and there, but never collapsing. This time, before the chariots might withdraw again, the final stage of the drama was enacted. The Roman commander had sized up the Celtic method of attack, and now acted as he thought fit. There was a long thin scream on the trumpet, and from either side of the cohorts came the galloping of hooves and the high wild shouting of the little Scythians, their sheepskin hats bobbing in the wind, their bows ready bent, their barbed arrows already flying into the whirling mass of the disorganized chariots. Gwydion saw his father go down, and watched the Romans run forward to him, thrusting with their javelins again and again, as the Scythians swept round and round, shooting as the desire took them now, at all fugitives. Math saw the king's chariot swing round, the red banner trailing tattered behind it, and gallop fast towards the brow of the hill. A few Scythian horsemen tried to follow it, but they were dragged from their ponies by equally savage tribesmen who formed a rearguard after their defeated master. Then Math heard Gwydion give a great sob and a shout, and saw that he was running down towards the thick of the battle. He did the only thing a friend could do, and followed him, Bel now running free at his side, his thong-lead dragging behind him.

Caratacus escaped from the battle but was betrayed to the Romans by Cartimandua, Queen of the Brigantes. He was taken to Rome to the emperor Claudius who spared his life.

During the next fifty years, in spite of the revolt of Boadicea, Queen of the Iceni, the Romans steadily advanced their control over the whole of England and Wales. At each stage they built forts to safeguard their conquests.

Often the Britons made surprise attacks and trapped the Romans in their forts. In this episode Marcus, a Roman commander, trapped inside Isca Dumniorum (Exeter) by a British attack, has given orders for a Roman counter-attack which he is leading himself.

Tortoise Attack

The great bars were drawn, and men stood ready to swing wide the heavy valves; and behind and on every side he had a confused impression of grim ranks massed to hold the gate, and draw them in again if ever they won back to it.

'Open up!' he ordered; and as the valves began to swing outward on their iron-shod posts, 'Form testudo.' His arm went up as he spoke, and through the whole column behind him he felt the movement echoed, heard the light kiss and click of metal on metal, as every man linked shield with his neighbour, to form the shield-roof which gave the formation its name. 'Now!'

The gates were wide; and like a strange many-legged beast, a gigantic woodlouse rather than a tortoise, the testudo was out across the causeway and heading straight downhill, its small, valiant cavalry wings spread on either side. The gates closed behind it, and from rampart and gate-tower anxious eyes watched it go. It had all been done so quickly that at the foot of the slope battle had only just joined, as the tribesmen hurled themselves yelling on the swiftly formed Roman square.

The testudo was not a fighting formation; but for rushing a position, for a break through, it had no equal. Also it had a strange and terrifying aspect that could be very useful. Its sudden appearance now, swinging down upon them with the whole weight of the hill behind it, struck a brief confusion into the swarming tribesmen. Only for a moment their wild ranks wavered and lost purpose; but in that moment the hard-pressed patrol saw it too, and with a hoarse shout came charging to join their comrades.

Down swept Marcus and his half Century, down and forward into the raging battle-mass of the enemy. They were slowed almost to a standstill, but never quite halted; once they were broken, but re-formed. A mailed wedge cleaving into the wild ranks of the tribesmen, until the moment came when the tortoise could serve them no longer; and above the turmoil Marcus shouted to the trumpeter beside him: 'Sound me "Break testudo".'

The clear notes of the trumpet rang through the uproar. The men lowered their shields, springing sideways to gain fighting space; and a flight of pilums hurtled into the swaying horde of tribesmen, spreading death and confusion wherever the iron heads struck. Then it was 'Out swords', and the charge driven home with a shout of 'Caesar! Caesar!' Behind them the valiant handful of cavalry were struggling to keep clear the line of retreat; in front, the patrol came grimly battling up to join them. But between them was still a living rampart of yelling, battle-frenzied warriors, amongst whom Marcus glimpsed again that figure with the horned moon on its forehead. He laughed, and sprang against them, his men storming behind him.

Patrol and relief force joined, and became one.

Instantly they began to fall back, forming as they did so a

roughly diamond formation that faced outward on all sides and was as difficult to hold as a wet pebble pressed between the fingers. The tribesmen thrust in on them from every side, but slowly, steadily, their short blades like a hedge of living, leaping steel, the cavalry breaking the way for them in wild rushes, they were drawing back towards the fortress gate— those that were left of them.

Back, and back. And suddenly the press was thinning, and Marcus, on the flank, snatched one glance over his shoulder, and saw the gate-towers very near, the swarming ranks of the defenders ready to draw them in. And in that instant there came a warning yelp of trumpets and a swelling thunder of hooves and wheels, as round the curve of the hill towards them, out of cover of the woodshore, swept a curved column of chariots.

Small wonder that the press had thinned.

The great battle-wains had long been forbidden to the tribes, and these were light chariots such as the one Marcus had driven two days ago, each carrying only a spearman beside the driver; but one horrified glance, as they hurtled nearer behind their thundering teams, was enough to show the wicked, whirling scythe-blades on the war-hubs of the wheels.

Close formation—now that their pilums were spent—was useless in the face of such a charge; again the trumpets yelped an order, and the ranks broke and scattered, running for the gateway, not in any hope of reaching it before the chariots were upon them, but straining heart and soul to gain the advantage of the high ground.

To Marcus, running with the rest, it seemed suddenly that there was no weight in his body, none at all. He was filled through and through with a piercing awareness of life and the sweetness of life held in his hollowed hand, to be tossed away like the shining balls that the children played with in the gardens of Rome. At the last instant, when the charge was almost upon them, he swerved aside from his men, out and back on his tracks, and flinging aside his sword, stood tensed to spring, full in the path of the oncoming chariots. In the breath of time that remained, his brain felt very cold and clear, and he seemed to have space to do quite a lot of thinking. If he sprang for the heads of the leading team, the odds were that he would merely be flung down and driven over without any check to the wild gallop. His best chance was to go for the charioteer. If he could bring him down, the whole team would be flung into confusion, and on that steep scarp the chariots coming behind would have difficulty in clearing the wreck. It was a slim chance, but if it came off it would gain for his men those few extra moments that might mean life or death. For himself, it was death. He was quite clear about that.

They were right upon him, a thunder of hooves that seemed to fill the universe; black manes streaming against the sky; the team that he had called his brothers, only two days ago. He hurled his shield clanging among them, and side-stepped, looking up into the grey face of Cradoc, the charioteer. For one splinter of time their eyes met in something that was almost a salute, a parting salute between two who might have been friends; then Marcus leapt in under the spearman's descending thrust, upward and sideways across the chariot bow. His weight crashed on to the reins, whose ends, after the British fashion, were wrapped about the charioteer's waist, throwing the team into instant chaos; his arms were round Cradoc, and they went half down together. His ears were full of the sound of rending timber and the hideous scream of a horse. Then sky and earth changed places, and with his hold still unbroken, he was flung down under the trampling hooves, under the scythe-bladed wheels and the collapsing welter of the overset chariot; and the jagged darkness closed over him.

As the country became more peaceful, important public buildings were constructed in the towns—a market place, temples, law courts, baths, even an amphitheatre where the gladiatorial games were held. The largest amphitheatre in the Roman world was the Colosseum at Rome which could hold over 50,000 spectators. The one which Marcus is now described as going to was much smaller but would be able to hold all the men from the Roman fort and many more Britons besides.

Gladiators

Whatever else of Rome the British had not taken to, they seemed to have taken to the Games with a vengeance, Marcus

Caesar and the Roman Conquest of Britain

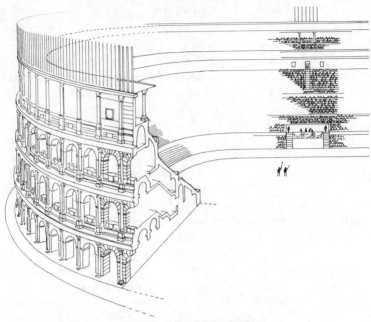

THE COLOSSEUM

The gladiators are saluting the emperor and his special guests in the imperial box before the fight with the words 'Hail, emperor, greetings from men about to die!' (Ave, imperator, morituri te salutant!)

The Colosseum was opened by the Emperor Titus in A.D. 80 and took its name from the colossal statue of the emperor Nero which stood nearby. It could hold at least 50,000 spectators and an intricate system of stairways approached through 76 numbered entrances led the spectators to their seats. The seats stretched right round the arena in an oval shape. The arena in the centre where the gladiators fought was composed of sand (harena is the Latin word for sand) to mop up the blood and afford the gladiators firmer footing. An awning could be stretched from the poles at the top of the amphitheatre to protect the audience from the sun.

Can you see which types of Greek columns have been used for the outside walls?

thought, looking about him at the crowded benches where townsfolk and tribesmen with their womenfolk and children jostled and shoved and shouted after the best places. There was a fair sprinkling of legionaries from the transit camp, and Marcus's quick glance picked out a bored young tribune sitting with several British lads all pretending to be equally Roman and equally bored. He remembered Colosseum crowds, chattering, shouting, quarrelling, laying bets and eating sticky

104

sweets. The British took their pleasures a little less loudly, to be sure, but on almost every face was the same eager, almost greedy look that the faces of the Colosseum crowds had worn.

A small disturbance near him drew Marcus's attention to the arrival of a family who were just entering their places on the Magistrates' benches a little to his right. A British family of the ultra-Roman kind, a large, good-natured-looking man, running to fat as men do who have been bred to a hard life and take to living soft instead; a woman with a fair and rather foolish face, prinked out in what had been the height of fashion in Rome two years ago—and very cold she must be, Marcus thought, in that thin mantle; and a girl of perhaps twelve or thirteen, with a sharply pointed face that seemed all golden eyes in the shadow of her dark hood. The stout man and Uncle Aquila saluted each other across the heads between, and the woman bowed. All Rome was in that bow; but the girl's eyes were fixed on the arena with a kind of horrified expectancy.

When the new-comers were settled in their places, Marcus touched his uncle's wrist, and cocked an inquiring eyebrow.

'A fellow Magistrate of mine, Kaeso by name, and his wife Valaria,' Uncle Aquila said. 'Incidentally, they are our next-door neighbours.'

'Are they so? But the little maiden; she is no bud of their branch, surely?'

But he got no answer to his question then, for at that moment a great crashing of cymbals and a fanfare of trumpets announced that the Games were about to begin. All round the crowded circus there was a sudden quietness and a craning forward. Again the trumpets sounded. The double doors at the far side were flung open, and out from their underground lodgements a double file of gladiators came marching into the arena, each carrying the weapons he would use later in the show. Shout on shout greeted their appearance. For a small colonial circus they seemed rather a good lot, Marcus thought, watching them as they paraded round the arena; too good, maybe, though probably they were all slaves. Marcus was something of a heretic where the Games were concerned; he liked well enough to see a wild-beast show, or a sham fight if it were well done, but to put up men—even slaves—to fight to the death for a crowd's amusement, seemed to him a waste.

GLADIATORS

The Retiarius (the 'Fisher') is armed with a trident and a net. Notice the leather or metal guard on his left shoulder. What else does he wear?

The Secutor (the 'Chaser') is armed with a dagger, helmet, shield, greave (on the left leg only) and leather arm bands (on his right arm only).

Gladiators

The men had halted now, before the Magistrates' benches; and in the few moments that they stood there, Marcus's whole attention was caught by one of them: a sword-and-buckler man of about his own age. He was rather short for a Briton, but powerful. His russet-brown hair, flung back by the savage pride with which he carried his head, showed the clipped ear that branded him for a slave. Seemingly he had been taken in war, for his breast and shoulders—he was stripped to the waist—were tattooed with blue warrior patterns. But it was none of these things that Marcus saw, only the look in the wide-set grey eyes that strained back at him out of the gladiator's young sullen face.

'This man is afraid,' said something deep in Marcus. 'Afraid —afraid,' and his own stomach cringed within him.

A score of weapons flashed in the wintry light as they were tossed up with a shout and caught again, and the gladiators wheeled and strode on down the wide curve that led back to their starting point. But the look that he had seen in the young swordsman's eyes remained with Marcus.

The first item on the programme was a fight between wolves and a brown bear. The bear did not want to fight, and was driven into battle by the long curling whip-lashes of the attendants. Presently, amid a great shouting from the onlookers, it was killed. Its body was dragged away, and with it the bodies of two wolves it had slain; the others were decoyed back into their wheeled cage for another time, and attendants spread fresh sand over the blood in the arena. Marcus glanced, without quite knowing why, at the girl in the dark hood, and saw her sitting as though frozen, her eyes wide and blank with horror in an ashy face. Still oddly shaken by that queer moment of contact with the young gladiator who was so very much afraid, he was filled with a sudden unreasoning anger against Kaeso and his wife for bringing the little maiden to see a thing like this, against all Games and all mobs who came to watch them with their tongues hanging out for horrors, even against the bear for being killed.

The next item was a sham fight, with little damage done save a few flesh wounds. (In the back of beyond, circus masters could not afford to be wasteful with their gladiators.) Then a boxing match in which the heavy cestus round the fighters' hands drew considerably more blood than the swords had done. A pause came, in which the arena was once again cleaned up and freshly sanded; and then a long gasp of expectancy ran through the crowd, and even the bored young tribune sat up and began to take some notice, as, with another blare of trumpets, the double doors swung wide once more, and two figures stepped out side by side into the huge emptiness of the arena. Here was the real thing: a fight to the death.

At first sight the two would seem to be unequally armed, for while one carried sword and buckler, the other, a slight dark man with something of the Greek in his face and build, carried only a three-pronged spear, and had over his shoulder a many-folded net, weighted with small discs of lead. But in truth, as Marcus knew only too well, the odds were all in favour of the man with the net, the Fisher, as he was called, and he saw with an odd sinking of the heart that the other was the young swordsman who was afraid.

'Never did like the net,' Uncle Aquila was grumbling. 'Not a clean fight, no!' A few moments earlier, Marcus had known that his damaged leg was beginning to cramp horribly; he had been shifting, and shifting again, trying to ease the pain without catching his uncle's notice, but now, as the two men crossed to the centre of the arena, he had forgotten about it.

The roar which greeted the pair of fighters had fallen to a breathless hush. In the centre of the arena the two men were being placed by the captain of the gladiators; placed with exquisite care, ten paces apart, with no advantage of light or wind allowed to either. The thing was quickly and competently done, and the captain stepped back to the barriers. For what seemed a long time, neither of the two moved. Moment followed moment, and still they remained motionless, the centre of all that great circle of staring faces. Then, very slowly, the swordsman began to move. Never taking his eyes from his adversary, he slipped one foot in front of the other; crouching a little, covering his body with the round buckler, inch by inch he crept forward, every muscle tensed to spring when the time came.

The Fisher stood as still as ever, poised on the balls of his feet, the trident in his left hand, his right lost in the folds of the net. Just beyond reach of the net, the swordsman checked

for a long, agonizing moment, and then sprang in. His attack
was so swift that the flung net flew harmlessly over his head,
and the Fisher leapt back and sideways to avoid his thrust,
then whirled about and ran for his life, gathering his net for
another cast as he ran, with the young swordsman hard behind
him. Half round the arena they sped, running low; the swordsman had not the other's length and lightness of build, but he
ran as a hunter runs—perhaps he had run down deer on the
hunting trail, before ever his ear was clipped—and he was
gaining on his quarry now. The two came flying round the
curve of the barrier towards the Magistrates' benches, and just
abreast of them the Fisher whirled about and flung once more.
The net whipped out like a dark flame; it licked round the
running swordsman, so intent on his chase that he had forgotten to guard for it; the weight carried the deadly folds across
and across again, and a howl burst from the crowd as he
crashed headlong and rolled over, helplessly meshed as a fly in
a spider's web.

Marcus wrenched forward, his breath caught in his throat.
The swordsman was lying just below him, so near that they
could have spoken to each other in an undertone. The Fisher
was standing over his fallen antagonist, with the trident poised
to strike, a little smile on his face, though his breath whistled
through widened nostrils, as he looked about him for the
bidding of the crowd. The fallen man made as though to raise
his hampered arm in the signal by which a vanquished
gladiator might appeal to the crowd for mercy; then let it drop
back, proudly, to his side. Through the fold of the net across
his face, he looked up straight into Marcus's eyes, a look as
direct and intimate as though they had been the only two
people in all that great amphitheatre.

Marcus was up and standing with one hand on the barrier
rail to steady himself, while with the other he made the sign
for mercy. Again and again he made it, with a blazing
vehemence, with every atom of will-power that was in him,
his glance thrusting like a challenge along the crowded tiers of
benches where already the thumbs were beginning to turn
down. This mob, this unutterably stupid, blood-greedy mob
that must somehow be swung over into forgoing the blood
it wanted! His gorge rose against them, and there was an

Caesar and the Roman Conquest of Britain

extraordinary sense of battle in him that could not have been more vivid had he been standing over the fallen gladiator, sword in hand. Thumbs up! *Thumbs up!* you fools! ... He had been aware from the first of Uncle Aquila's great thumb pointing skyward beside him; suddenly he was aware of a few others echoing the gesture, and then a few more. For a long, long moment the swordsman's fate still hung in the balance, and then as thumb after thumb went up, the Fisher slowly lowered his trident and with a little mocking bow, stepped back.

Marcus drew a shuddering breath, and relaxed into a flood of pain from his cramped leg, as an attendant came forward to disentangle the swordsman and aid him to his feet. He did not look at the young gladiator again. This moment was shame for him, and Marcus felt that he had no right to witness it.

That evening, over the usual game of draughts, Marcus asked his uncle: 'What will become of that lad now?'

Uncle Aquila moved an ebony piece after due consideration. 'The young fool of a swordsman? He will be sold in all likelihood. The crowd do not pay to see a man fight, when once he has been down and at their mercy.'

'That is what I have been thinking,' Marcus said. He looked up from making his own move. 'How do prices run in these parts? Would fifteen hundred sesterces buy him?'

'Very probably. Why?'

'Because I have that much left of my pay and a parting thank-offering that I had from Tullus Lepidus. There was not much to spend it on in Isca Dumnoniorum.'

Uncle Aquila's brows cocked inquiringly. 'Are you suggesting buying him yourself?'

'Would you give him house-room?'

'I expect so,' said Uncle Aquila. 'Though I am somewhat at a loss to understand why you should wish to keep a tame gladiator. Why not try a wolf instead?'

Marcus laughed. 'It is not so much a tame gladiator as a body-slave that I need. I cannot go on overworking poor old Stephanos for ever.'

Uncle Aquila leaned across the chequered board. 'And what makes you think that an ex-gladiator would make you a suitable body-slave?'

110

Suggested Activities

'To speak the truth, I had not thought about it,' Marcus said. 'How do you advise me to set about buying him?'

'Send down to the circus slave-master, and offer half of what you expect to pay. And sleep with a knife under your pillow thereafter,' said Uncle Aquila.

The Romans had conquered England and Wales by the end of the first century A.D. *but the tribes of the Picts and Scots in southern Scotland often invaded the Roman territory. The problem was finally solved when the Roman Emperor Hadrian built a wall across the North of England. The fortresses and towns of Roman Britain had been connected by a network of roads and these were extended to the wall. These fortifications kept Britain safe so that she became more prosperous and more civilized than she had ever been. However, in about* A.D. *400 the Roman legions were called back to help Rome which was threatened by invasions of barbarian tribes. In* A.D. *410 Rome was captured by the Goths and the legions never returned to Britain. Soon after Britain too was overcome by the invasions of foreign tribes, the Picts, Scots, Jutes, Angles and Saxons, but many Roman roads and much of Hadrian's wall still stand today to remind us of the peace and prosperity which the Romans gave to Britain for 300 years.*

Suggested Activities

Writing

1. Imagine you were the standard bearer who inspired the Romans to attack the British. Describe Caesar's landing and the part you played in it.

2. Produce a newspaper coming out on the evening of the Ides of March. Include contributions made by Caesar's friends and his enemies giving eyewitness accounts of his death, an obituary, pictures, latest news, what might happen next, etc.

3. Describe the difference between the Roman and British methods of fighting. See pp. 88 and 94–100.

4. Tell the story of your fight as a gladiator in the amphitheatre.

111

5. Suppose Marcus did buy the gladiator who had been spared. Continue the story in your own way. Do you think Marcus had anything to be afraid of?

Drawing

1. Draw a picture of a Roman legionary with the names of his weapons and parts of his armour (see p. 86).
2. Draw a picture of Julius Caesar's army landing in Britain (see pp. 85–90) or the Roman army fighting against Caratacus.
3. Draw a picture of Julius Caesar (see p. 85) and if you can find them pictures of Roman emperors, for example Augustus, Nero, Trajan, Hadrian, Constantine, etc.
4. Draw a large panorama of the battle described on pp. 94–100.
5. Draw a picture of the gladiators' fight described on pp. 103–110.

Acting

1. Act the story of Caesar's death as described on pp. 92–93. The actors needed are Caesar, Brutus, Cassius, Metellus, Casca and Pompey's statue. All the rest of the class can be the Senate, who must stand up when Caesar comes in. Someone could narrate the story while it is acted.

Separate scenes could also be acted of what happened before Caesar came in to the Senate as in Shakespeare's play *Julius Caesar* (see pp. 90–92).

2. One person could be an interviewer questioning another one about what he saw and felt when Caesar was killed. Choose to be whichever character you like—even Pompey's statue or Caesar's ghost, or just one of the Senate.

Finding Out

1. Find out what other kinds of soldiers there were in the Roman Army besides legionaries. How were they armed and how did they work together in battle? (See pp. 96–99.)
2. Find out about some Roman emperors. Try looking up Augustus, Nero, Trajan, Hadrian and Constantine. Draw

pictures of them, write down their dates and some of the important things they did.

3. Find out what you can about Caratacus and Boadicea who led the Britons in their fight for freedom.

4. Did the Romans make any impression on your area? Are there any Roman roads or forts? Can you find any inscriptions on tombstones or old buildings in Latin (the language of the Romans)? See if your local museum has any Roman remains. Try to gather as much information as you can about the Romans and make it into a book.

5. Find out why the Romans considered it so important to build good roads throughout their empire. Describe with diagrams how they were built and draw a map of the Roman network of roads in Britain. Show how road building has developed from this to the present day.

Further Reading

A. Duggan, *Julius Caesar*; *Romans*.
Irwin Isenberg, *Caesar*, Cassell Caravel series.
J. Liversidge, *Roman Britain*, Then and There series.
L. Du Garde Peach, *Julius Caesar and Roman Britain*, Ladybird book.
E. Royston Pike, *Republican Rome*, Young Historian series.
Stephanie Plowman, *To Spare the Conquered*.
R. R. Sellman, *Roman Britain*, Methuen Outlines series.
William Shakespeare, *Julius Caesar*.
Rosemary Sutcliff, *Eagle of the Ninth*; *Outcast*; *The Silver Branch*.
D. Taylor, *Ancient Rome*, Methuen Outlines series.
O. Thompson, *The Romans in Scotland*, Then and There series.
Geoffrey Trease, *Word to Caesar*.
Henry Treece, *Legions of the Eagle*; *The Queen's Brooch*.

6 Life in the Roman Empire

The Britons soon adopted Roman customs and a Roman way of life. Houses were built in the Roman style, especially large country houses which the Romans called villas. In the following story Paul, a Briton, tells of how he visits such a villa for the first time with a Roman poet called Severus.

Visit to a Villa

We stepped out of the carriage. The house was built round three sides of a square, long and low, with a pillared verandah on the ground floor and half-timbered walls rising for the upper storey. There must be dozens of rooms altogether, though one wing was probably just for the slaves.

We had evidently been sighted as we came up the road, for we had hardly set foot to the ground when three figures came hurrying from the front door.

'Severus! My dear fellow——'

'Severus! Are you safe? We heard such dreadful rumours! But why didn't you send us word? No opportunity? But why?'

Veranius was a ruddy-cheeked, stalwart country gentleman, and his boots suggested that he had only just dismounted from a ride round his estate.

Veranius' wife, Matidia, and his daughter, Julia, are introduced, but Matidia talks so much that he wants to get his visitors away from her.

Veranius rescued us in the only possible manner, by leading us off to the bathroom to remove the dust of travel. Severus's personal slave appeared, a Greek named Curio, whose mild dark eyes lit up affectionately at the sight of his master. The four of us escaped to the baths in the east wing.

A ROMAN DINNER

To eat their meals the Romans reclined on couches arranged in groups of three to form three sides of a square with tables in the middle. The main meal, dinner, would start about 3 pm and might last for several hours.

On formal occasions like this Romans would wear a toga like the host who is welcoming a guest in the picture. The Roman toga was made out of a semi-circular piece of material about 6 yards by 2 yards. One end of it nearly touched the ground in front. The other end was thrown over the left shoulder, brought round under the right arm and again thrown over the left shoulder. Only Roman citizens might wear the toga; the slave carrying the tray in the picture wears a tunic. The Roman wore a tunic under his toga.

The floor and walls would be decorated with brightly coloured pictures or designs in mosaic or marble.

115

'Nothing very luxurious,' Veranius apologized—though to me the tinted marble columns and the mosaic floors were the finest I had ever seen. 'My wife says it's a disgrace—she says she has to go down into the town for a civilized bath.'

'Perhaps,' suggested Severus, 'there is a better flow of gossip there—if not of hot water?'

'Maybe.' Veranius chuckled. 'She does like to meet the other ladies, of course.'

The two men talked while Curio rubbed us down and brought in clean clothes. Severus did not put on a fresh toga. Indoors, he was content with his tunics. I was lent the gayest of them all, yellow—'to match your hair, sir,' Curio murmured with a smile—and decorated with the double purple stripe which anybody could wear now, though once it had been a sign of rank.

Veranius asked about the trouble in the north, ugly rumours of which had filtered down to him. Severus countered with inquiries about the farm, and it was easy to see, from the way out host's eyes lit up, where his main interests lay.

Veranius (I found out later—his wife soon told me) was descended from British princes who had fought against Julius Caesar. But he himself was a peace-loving man, thoroughly romanized, with no hankering after the old days. Roman ideas, he knew, had revolutionized farming, and he had no patience with those who would not learn them. A man of few words, mostly, as he had to be, Veranius could wax eloquent on the one, many-sided, subject of his estate. His cherry-trees, his scheme to drain the marshland or to lighten a clay soil with sand, his bee-hives, his herb-garden, his hopes of making wine from his own grapes...

'And another thing!' (I remember him once exclaiming at dinner, much to his wife's annoyance.) 'Manure! That's the most valuable thing we've learnt about from you Romans! Don't tell me about straight roads and hot water! What really——'

'Veranius!' Matidia had quenched him with a look. 'I do wish you wouldn't talk about "you Romans". As if we weren't *all*.'

Matidia was not only a scold and a chatterbox, she was a snob. She made Severus welcome because she knew he was a famous poet from Rome, though she had not the wit to see the point in his verses. Having him in the house gave her social standing with the neighbours.

She aped all the fashionable customs of the capital, so far as she could learn them at such a distance. When we went into dinner, that first evening, I saw to my dismay that we were even expected to eat in Roman style.

Big sloping couches, all gilt and ivory, were drawn up on three sides of the table. There were no chairs or stools. Not only was Matidia herself proposing to recline, like the men, on one plump elbow, but even we young people were evidently expected to do the same. I had never done so in my life— Father would have had a fit if he could have seen me at that fantastic dinner-party—but if young Julia could manage, I reckoned I could.

There were no other guests. Matidia kept apologizing, saying she would have brought in some friends to fill up the table if she had known we were coming. As it was, the three grown-ups stretched themselves side by side, and Julia and I were put to face them across the table. The other couch was empty, and of course the fourth side of the table was left clear anyhow, so that the slaves could reach it with their dishes.

It was a wonderful meal, I will say that. We started with oysters, lettuce, and hard-boiled eggs. Then we went on to the main course, with chicken and lamb and salmon and some other things I did not try. Finally, after the slaves had been round again to wash our hands for us, and Veranius had made a little thank-offering to the guardian spirits of the home, we had little cakes and fruit, some of it fresh from the estate but some, the dried figs and the dates, brought from the far side of the Empire.

Julia watched me like a cat throughout the meal. She must have seen me fumble and hesitate occasionally. I had to think quickly about one or two little things, like slipping my cushion under my left side to support me comfortably, and spreading my napkin to protect the couch from spots of gravy. And, of course, those oysters. But, by keeping my eye on the others, I got through pretty well, and I held out my sticky fingers for the slave to pour the jug over them as if I'd been doing it every night of my life for years.

Afterwards, because the evening was warm, we all sat in the portico, watching the western sky fade from orange to apple-green and then violet.

Matidia gabbled on and on, more than ever like a fountain. Veranius was sleepy after a long day in his fields. Severus, as always, was polite.

Julia and I sat a few feet away. There was a pillar between us and the others. Julia said:

'We have ever so many horses. Would you like to see them?'

'Very much.'

Later Paul goes into the nearby town (Bath).

The town itself is only a small one—there is no garrison, no government offices, and no trade to speak of—but people come to it as a health resort from all over the province, and even from the Continent. The baths are quite magnificent— the main pool is about eighty feet by forty, surrounded by colonnades, with forty-foot pillars soaring overhead. There are beautiful wall-paintings and mosaic pictures on the floors, made up of thousands of coloured pieces exquisitely put together, and shining bronze statues and pink-veined marble slabs, silver lamps, and goodness knows what else. But to me the most wonderful thing was to see the water itself, steaming as it gushed out of its lead pipe, and to know that no human hand had stoked a fire to heat it.

Of course, much as we enjoyed the swimming and diving, the lazy floating and the massage afterwards, we did not go down into the town just for that.

The baths were a sort of club. We met some of the same visitors every day and made friends with them, and most days there was at least one newcomer with the latest news from the outside world.

The Britons imitated Rome but could not possibly equal her. Rome had over a million inhabitants, almost as much as the total population of Britain. The road traffic was so great that it was banned during the day to allow pedestrians to walk through. The traffic was allowed in from dusk to dawn, but the noise kept many of the inhabitants awake all night. There were many

An Hour at the Races

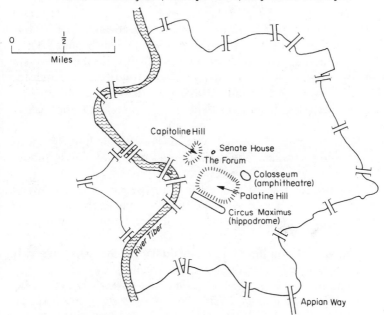

ROME

at the time of Augustus, showing the walls, the gates and the bridges

market places, temples and baths much larger than any to be found in Britain. The amphitheatre called the Colosseum could hold 50,000 spectators. There was also a hippodrome where the chariot races were held, capable of holding 150,000 spectators. In the following description Paul and Tonia, a Roman boy and girl, go to the chariot races to support a friend of theirs, Manlius. Paul tells the story.

An Hour at the Races

The restless horses edged at last into a reasonable line. The white cloth fluttered down to the sand below, the trumpet blared—and they were off!

About two hundred thousand people promptly took leave of their senses. Or so it seemed.

'Come on, the Greens!'

'White—come on, White!'

'Red! Good old Reds!'

'Show 'em, the Blues!'

The course was a long narrow oval of sparkling, gritty sand. Down the centre ran a marble barrier, decorated with statues and ending in two turning-posts of gilded bronze. These turning-posts produced the biggest thrills in the race—the chariots had to wheel so sharply, and a fraction of an inch too near might mean an upset, a driver thrown headlong, or a wheel torn from its axle. Then, too, there was the risk of collision with another chariot.

'Oh, come *on*, Manlius!' wailed Tonia. Her knuckles were white with anguish. She was bobbing up and down as though she herself were in the race.

But Manlius's new team was lying well back. There was a Red driver in the lead, then a Green and one of the other Blues fighting for second place, and two others strung out in front of my friend.

The signal-dolphins lining the embankment were turned to show that it was now the sixth lap, the last but one. . . .

'Manlius!' Tonia was screaming. She could have saved her breath. He had gained a trifle, but he was still only fifth. He had not a hope. From the odds that the bookmakers had been calling they must have known it all along. She might have saved her money as well as her breath, I reflected sulkily. I agreed with her father more heartily than ever. Betting was the ruin of the Roman character. The passion to get something for nothing—or almost nothing—would drive people to the silliest behaviour.

The Green driver was overhauling the Red. The crowd was nearly delirious. The Green was using his whip like a maniac. He cut in riskily, too riskily. . . . A tremendous howl went up from the stands.

'Shipwreck! SHIPWRECK!'

For an instant the two chariots seemed locked together. A man shot out, a green tunic rolled over in the sand, a loose wheel ran wobbling away like a child's hoop——

The man behind me swore violently. Both chariots were out of the race. Green was unhurt, but by the time he had cut himself free from his reins it was far too late for him to regain control of his team. And it was poor Red who had lost a wheel.

120

CIRCUS MAXIMUS

The Circus Maximus (the 'Greatest Circuit') at Rome where chariot races were staged could hold at least 150,000 spectators. The four-horsed chariots raced 7 laps round a central reservation called the spina (the 'spine') decorated with statues and shrines. There were four teams of horses each distinguished by a colour (red, white, green or blue). The cornering was most important and dangerous. The charioteer had to hold back the inner horse and give the reins to the outer horse at just the right moment to keep as close as possible to the turning post and avoid losing ground.

121

The other chariots came thundering on behind. The attendants prepared to turn the bronze dolphin. Last lap!

'Blue! Come on, Blue!'

'Manlius!'

I could scarcely believe my eyes. It had been one of the other Blue drivers, surely, in third place? But now Manlius was coming up, hand over fist. Out of the flying dust shot the four outstretched heads, and erect above them, serene as a god in the clouds, Manlius!

Tonia clutched my wrist as he neared the turning-post. She was so frantic, her nails dug into me. I was not exactly calm myself. He could never do it—he could never make the sharp left-handed turn at that appalling speed. It was too much to ask of the trace-horses, the stallions on the outside. One must almost stop and act as the pivot, and the other had such a wide arc through which to swing.

They thundered on, those four silky bays, each with the Libyan star clear on its forehead. Manlius cracked his whip, but I could swear that he did not touch them with it. I closed my eyes as they came to the turn——

'Shipwreck!' The howl went up from a hundred thousand supporters of his rivals.

'No! He's got by!'

The chariot must almost have scraped the post. But his blue tunic was flashing down the straight for the last time. The next team was thirty yards behind. The roar of the crowd must have been heard on the other side of the Tiber.

'Blue wins! Manlius! Manlius!'

Tonia let go my wrist. 'Here,' I began, 'where are you off to?' But she had vanished, leaving me to study her nail-prints on my flesh. In a few minutes she came pushing her way back to me.

'The odds were very good,' she whispered triumphantly. 'No one else seemed to think he could possibly win.' She slipped me a great handful of money. 'Do look after all this, I'm scared of thieves now.'

'Come on,' I said sternly, jumping to my feet. 'We're going. Before you risk it all on some driver whose nose you fancy.'

'Yes, Paul.' She followed me with surprising meekness. 'But you needn't worry, I shall never, never want to bet again.'

'Good.'

'It's far, far too upsetting.'

We walked out into the street and looked for a cab-rank. A few minutes later we were in a hired carriage, bowling along the Appian Way.

We know about life in Rome and the hundreds of other smaller cities in the Roman Empire, each with its own market place, temples, baths and amphitheatre, because one of them, Pompeii, has been preserved to this day almost exactly as it was. Pompeii was five miles away from the Volcano Vesuvius. For

THE ERUPTION OF MOUNT VESUVIUS

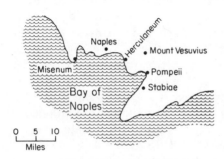

centuries Mount Vesuvius had been dormant but in A.D. *62 it suddenly erupted, destroying many of the buildings. The inhabitants worked hard to rebuild it. Then in* A.D. *79 it erupted again. Pliny was a Roman writer, who happened to be staying nearby at Misenum, nineteen miles away. Later he wrote a letter to a friend telling him about the eruption.*

The Eruption of Vesuvius: An Eye-Witness Account

After my uncle's departure I spent the rest of the day with my books, as this was my reason for staying behind. Then I took a bath, dined, and then dozed fitfully for a while. For several days past there had been earth tremors which were not particularly alarming because they are frequent in Campania: but that night the shocks were so violent that everything felt as if it were not only shaken but overturned. My mother hurried into my room and found me already getting up to wake her if she were still asleep. We sat down in the forecourt of the house, between the buildings and the sea close by. I don't know whether I should call this courage or folly on my part (I was only seventeen at the time) but I called for a volume of Livy and went on reading as if I had nothing else to do. I even went on with the extracts I had been making. Up came a friend of my uncle's who had just come from Spain to join him. When he saw us sitting there and me actually reading, he scolded us both—me for my foolhardiness and my mother for allowing it. Nevertheless, I remained absorbed in my book.

By now it was dawn, but the light was still dim and faint. The buildings round us were already tottering, and the open space we were in was too small for us not to be in real and imminent danger if the house collapsed. This finally decided us to leave the town. We were followed by a panic-stricken mob of people wanting to act on someone else's decision in preference to their own (a point in which fear looks like prudence), who hurried us on our way by pressing hard behind in a dense crowd. Once beyond the buildings we stopped, and there we had some extraordinary experiences which thoroughly alarmed us. The carriages we had ordered to be brought out began to run in different directions though the ground was quite level, and would not remain stationary even when wedged with stones. We also saw the sea sucked away and apparently forced back by the earthquake: at any rate it receded from the shore so that quantities of sea creatures were left stranded on dry sand. On the landward side a fearful black cloud was rent by forked and quivering bursts of flame, and parted to reveal great tongues of fire, like flashes of lightning magnified in size.

At this point my uncle's friend from Spain spoke up still more urgently: 'If your brother, if your uncle is still alive, he will want you both to be saved; if he is dead, he would want you to survive him—why put off your escape?' We replied that we would not think of considering our own safety as long as we were uncertain of his. Without waiting any longer, our friend rushed off and hurried out of danger as fast as he could.

Soon afterwards the cloud sank down to earth and covered the sea; it had already blotted out Capri and hidden the promontory of Misenum from sight. Then my mother implored, entreated and commanded me to escape as best I could—a young man might escape, whereas she was old and slow and could die in peace as long as she had not been the cause of my death too. I refused to save myself without her, and grasping her hand forced her to quicken her pace. She gave in reluctantly, blaming herself for delaying me. Ashes were already falling, not as yet very thickly. I looked round: a dense black cloud was coming up behind us, spreading over the earth like a flood. 'Let us leave the road while we can still see,' I said, 'or we shall be knocked down and trampled underfoot in the dark by the crowd behind.' We had scarcely sat down to rest when darkness fell, not the dark of a moonless or cloudy night, but as if the lamp had been put out in a closed room. You could hear the shrieks of women, the wailing of infants, and the shouting of men; some were calling their parents, others their children or their wives, trying to recognize them by their voices. People bewailed their own fate or that of their relatives, and there were some who prayed for death in their terror of dying. Many besought the aid of the gods, but still more imagined there were no gods left, and that the universe was plunged into eternal darkness for evermore. There were people, too, who added to the real perils by inventing fictitious dangers: some reported that part of Misenum had collapsed or another part was on fire, and though their tales were false they found others to believe them. A gleam of light returned, but we took this to be a warning of the approaching flames rather than daylight. However, the flames remained some distance off; then darkness came on once more and ashes began to fall again, this time in heavy showers. We rose from time to time and shook them off, otherwise we should have been buried and crushed beneath their weight. I could boast that not a groan or cry of fear escaped me in these perils, had I not derived some poor consolation in my mortal lot from the belief that the whole world was dying with me and I with it.

At last the darkness thinned and dispersed like smoke or cloud; then there was genuine daylight, and the sun actually shone out, but yellowish as it is during an eclipse. We were terrified to see everything changed, buried deep in ashes like snowdrifts.

125

Pliny's uncle was in command of the Roman fleet at Misenum. In another letter Pliny described what happened to him.

The Eruption of Vesuvius: A Scientist Investigates

My uncle was stationed at Misenum, in active command of the fleet. On 24 August, in the early afternoon, my mother drew his attention to a cloud of unusual size and appearance. He had been out in the sun, had taken a cold bath and lunched while lying down, and was then working at his books. He called for

ROMAN HOUSE

The House of the Silver Wedding at Pompeii (so called because it was uncovered in 1893 when the royal family of Italy were celebrating their Silver Wedding). The atrium is in the foreground and the garden or peristyle is beyond. This is quite different to the villa (country house) described on page 114.

his shoes and climbed up to a place which would give him the best view of the phenomenon. It was not clear at that distance from which mountain the cloud was rising (it was afterwards known to be Vesuvius); its general appearance can best be expressed as being like an umbrella pine, for it rose to a great height on a sort of trunk and then split off into branches, I

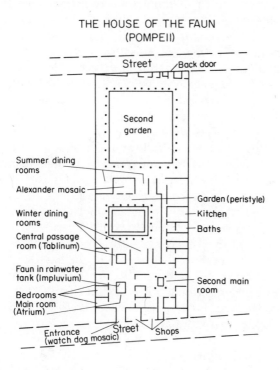

THE HOUSE OF THE FAUN
(POMPEII)

imagine because it was thrust upwards by the first blast and then left unsupported as the pressure subsided, or else it was borne down by its own weight so that it spread out and gradually dispersed. In places it looked white, elsewhere blotched and dirty, according to the amount of soil and ashes it carried with it. My uncle's scholarly acumen saw at once that it was important enough for a closer inspection, and he ordered a boat to be made ready, telling me I could come with him if I wished. I replied that I preferred to go on with my studies, and as it happened he had himself given me some writing to do.

As he was leaving the house he was handed a message from Rectina, wife of Tascus whose house was at the foot of the mountain, so that escape was impossible except by boat. She was terrified by the danger threatening her and implored him to rescue her from her fate. He changed his plans, and what he had begun in a spirit of inquiry he completed as a hero. He gave orders for the warships to be launched and went on board himself with the intention of bringing help to many more people besides Rectina, for this lovely stretch of coast was thickly populated. He hurried to the place which everyone else was hastily leaving, steering his course straight for the danger zone. He was entirely fearless, describing each new movement and phase of the portent to be noted down exactly as he observed them. Ashes were already falling, hotter and thicker as the ships drew near, followed by bits of pumice and blackened stones, charred and cracked by the flames: then suddenly they were in shallow water, and the shore was blocked by the debris from the mountain. For a moment my uncle wondered whether to turn back, but when the helmsman advised this he refused, telling him that Fortune stood by the courageous and they must make for Pomponianus at Stabiae. He was cut off there by the breadth of the bay (for the shore gradually curves round a basin filled by the sea) so that he was not as yet in danger, though it was clear that this would come nearer as it spread. Pomponianus had therefore already put his belongings on board ship, intending to escape if the contrary wind fell. This wind was of course full in my uncle's favour, and he was able to bring his ship in. He embraced his terrified friend, cheered and encouraged him, and thinking he could calm his fears by showing his own composure, gave orders that he was to be carried to the bathroom. After his bath he lay down and dined; he was quite cheerful, or at any rate he pretended he was, which was no less courageous.

Meanwhile on Mount Vesuvius broad sheets of fire and leaping flames blazed at several points, their bright glare emphasized by the darkness of night. My uncle tried to allay the fears of his companions by repeatedly declaring that these were nothing but bonfires left by the peasants in their terror, or else empty houses on fire in the districts they had abandoned. Then he went to rest and certainly slept, for as he was a stout man his breathing was rather loud and heavy and could be heard by people coming and going outside his door. By this time the courtyard giving access to his room was full of ashes mixed with pumice-stones, so that its level had risen, and if he had stayed in the room any longer he would never have got out. He was wakened, came out and joined Pomponianus and the rest of the household who had sat up all night. They debated whether to stay indoors or take their chance in the open, for the buildings were now shaking with violent shocks, and seemed to be swaying to and fro as if they were torn from their foundations. Outside on the other hand, there was the danger of falling pumice-stones, even though these were light and porous; however, after comparing the risks they chose the latter. In my uncle's case one reason outweighed the other, but for the others it was a choice of fears. As a protection against falling objects they put pillows on their heads tied down with cloths.

Elsewhere there was daylight by this time, but they were still in darkness, blacker and denser than any ordinary night, which they relieved by lighting torches and various kinds of lamp. My uncle decided to go down to the shore and investigate on the spot the possibility of any escape by sea, but he found the waves still wild and dangerous. A sheet was spread on the ground for him to lie down, and he repeatedly asked for cold water to drink. Then the flames and smell of sulphur which gave warning of the approaching fire drove the others to take flight and roused him to stand up. He stood leaning on two slaves and then suddenly collapsed, I imagine because the dense fumes choked his breathing by blocking his windpipe which was constitutionally weak and narrow and often inflamed. When daylight returned on the 26th—two days after the last day he had seen—his body was found intact and uninjured, still fully clothed and looking more like sleep than death.

Stabiae was ten miles away from the volcano. What was it like at Pompeii, half that distance? Very few lived to tell the tale as the following story shows.

Life in the Roman Empire

Beloved of the Gods[1]

And now it was the 24th August, that inauspicious day when the mundus[2] within the Forum was opened wide. Two aediles[3] dragged aside the stone that hid the entrance to the Underworld. They were amazed at the hot blast of air that rushed up to meet them, and staggered back, catching their breath. Early in the morning, the Lady Marcia, accompanied by Iris, went to the Temple of Isis to offer prayers. There had been no tremors for several hours, but Iris walked trembling by her side, as terrified by the unnatural events as Paulina's little marmoset, who had spent the last few days gibbering in fright. In the temple she stood beside her mistress as the Lady Marcia knelt before the statue of the goddess, attended by a priest who swung a censer and chanted a holy song.

It had been full sunlight when they left home; but now, outside the temple, a sudden darkness overcast the sky. It grew dusky as a summer night, and in that final moment all life, all movement, seemed to pause unbearably. Then, from Vesuvius itself there came a monstrous and appalling noise—the noise of the volcano in eruption. Once more the earth shook crazily, but this time for longer, and more violently, than it had ever done before. And from the whole surface of the ground, throughout the city, there arose that burning blast the aediles in the Forum had felt a little while before. That mighty crack split wide the very summit of the mountain; the heaving, broiling mass within the rock burst its bonds at last. From the crater there rushed forth smoke and flames and blazing mud, and fiery boulders hurtled into the air. The burning mud gushed down the mountainside as swiftly as a horse can gallop, in a tide of uncontrollable destruction. Villas and farms and vineyards, flocks of sheep and herds of cattle: all were swamped beneath the burning deluge. And as the dreadful flood rushed down towards the sea, showers of ashes fell thickly on the streets and buildings of Pompeii, glowing brightly in the darkness.

[1] 'He whom the gods love dies young,' says a Greek playwright, Menander (ὃν οἱ θεοὶ φιλοῦσιν ἀποθνῄσκει νέος).

[2] i.e. the entrance to the Underworld.

[3] Aediles were the magistrates in charge of public ceremonies.

EGGS, NUTS AND LENTILS

These were found in the temple of Isis at Pompeii and formed the priests' meal at the moment of the eruption.

This was that 'dire emergency' Antonius Piso and his fellow merchants had thought half-possible! This was the ultimate terror that the wretched Iris and her like had dreaded! This was the unimaginable holocaust presaged by the days of burning heat and quaking earth!

Now panic ruled the city. Those who remained—all those who could—fled through the streets, brushing the scorching ashes from their heads, dodging the hail of white-hot stones, urged on by man's deepest fear: fear of the elements beyond control, of chaos come to earth. Those who were weakest perished in the headlong rush; children lost their parents, and could not find them in the crowded, clamouring darkness. 'It is the ending of the world!' a frenzied voice shrieked above the throng. 'The gods have abandoned us!'

The Lord Aquila set forth at once to seek his wife within the Temple of Isis; but he struggled vainly against a rush of people moving in the opposite direction, and was carried helplessly along with them. A rider on a fear-crazed horse came trampling through the crowd; one of the horse's plunging hoofs struck the Lord Aquila on the head, and with a groan he slipped unconscious to the ground. No one paused to help him rise, and he was trampled underfoot.

Iris fled screaming from the temple the moment that the mountain cracked asunder; hard on her heels the priests themselves rushed forth from their inner sanctum, kilting their white robes above their knees. The Lady Marcia clung to the altar steps; and as the panic-stricken figures hurtled past her, she gasped to see that one had flung the goddess' gold and silver robe about his shoulders. Only the acolyte beside her stayed; he came to kneel upon the steps; and at the end, when the Lady Marcia's breath was mercifully stopped by the choking gases that accompanied the flow of scalding lava, she was not alone.

At the Calpurnian house, meanwhile, Tiro the steward ordered all the slaves to leave immediately. They were already scrambling out of doors and windows, fleeing they knew not where. The little marmoset clawed its way out with them, squealing pitifully and trailing its silver chain. It still wore Paulina's pearls dangling from its ears; someone in the crowd caught at the creature roughly and stripped them off. Callias knelt in the guest chamber beside Felicia, who lay upon her mattress clutching the Greek girl's hand, and gazing on her face in wordless terror. Agilis, seeking Callias throughout the house, burst into the little room at last.

'Come, Callias, come!' he cried. 'There is no time to linger!'

Bran panted by his side, straining forward on his chain. It was all Agilis could do to hold him.

Callias turned her head to look at Agilis. Her eyes were brimming over with tears. 'How can I leave Felicia?' she asked, imploringly. And yet she felt the prick of terror that urged her to fly from the house. She used to cringe before a lightning flash, and tremble at Mars' thunder in the sky. But that was as nothing beside the dreadful wrath now pouring down upon them from Vesuvius!

Agilis seized her roughly by the arm. 'There is no time, I tell you!' He tore her hand from Felicia's grasp, and the old woman uttered a thin shriek and raised herself upon her elbow. She looked at Callias and Agilis as they stood together in the doorway, and Callias sought her gaze pleadingly. Then Felicia shook her head; suddenly the awful terror left her eyes. 'Go, go while you can!' she told them. 'Agilis is right, my child. Life lies before you both. My life is over. A slave is only half a human being—and a crippled slave is less than that. If you see my son again, tell him I send a mother's blessing on his head!'

'Oh, it is hard to leave her there!' Callias cried as they ran out into the street. The burning ashes, settling in thick piles, scorched their ankles as they made their way along.

'Do you think we would have left her, if there had been the remotest chance of saving her?' demanded Agilis. 'It would be impossible to take a litter through these streets!'

They hurried on together, fleeing with the crowd. And the great dog, slavering with fear, led them unerringly towards the sea. Smouldering ash burnt Callias' face and forehead as she clung to Agilis' hand. They were making for the Porta Marina; and now they passed along the street where Antonius Piso's house was situated. A little way beyond it, Agilis' straining eyes caught sight of a struggle taking place between two figures; in the dim light he could just discern one man beating off another who had attacked him. A hoarse cry arose: 'Help, help! Good people, save me!' But none heeded it. None save

NARROW LANE AT POMPEII

Today called the Vico Storto (Crooked Alley).

Agilis, who swerved abruptly in his headlong rush, and ran to the man's side. The assailant was thick-set and vicious; more than a match for Agilis. But Bran was there, and at Agilis' command he leapt upon the man, who staggered back, clutching at his throat, then fled into the darkness.

'Are you all right?' Agilis asked, as he and Callias helped the victim to his feet. 'Why,' he cried, 'it is the wool merchant to whose shop I came with news of Felicia's accident!'

Antonius Piso's eyes opened wide as he recognized his rescuer. 'It is you!' he cried. 'My son! You have saved my life. That was a thief who saw me leave my shop holding my money-bags, and sought to rob and murder me. Even in this hour of disaster!'

Agilis slung one of the money-bags across his shoulder, and with Antonius still clasping the other one, the three of them continued on their way towards the shore, Bran snuffing eagerly as they approached the sea.

'We—must—find a boat!' Antonius panted as they hurried on. 'My gold will pay for it! All my gold if necessary!' And as he spoke he cast one fearful backward glance towards Vesuvius and the torrents of bubbling lava rushing ever nearer.

The crowd stampeded through the gateway to the sea; and even in their headlong flight, there were many who marvelled to see the Roman sentry steadfast at his post, unheeding of the rain of fire upon his plumed head, his spear held upright in his hand.

And now they reached the shore. The sea was heaving in its bed, throwing great waves upon the beach. Little groups of figures laboured to launch frail craft upon the water. Many overturned as soon as they were tossed upon the waves, and hundreds were drowned. Antonius and his companions were fortunate. They found a merchant craft about to leave the harbour; Antonius knew the master, who had often carried consignments of wool for him. Eyeing the merchant's money-bags, the master let them come on board, and the ship set out across the troubled sea, her sailors straining at the oars. Even upon the sea the shower of ash and stones rained continuously; blazing fragments fell hissing to the water all around them. The decks were crowded with survivors from the burning city—the city that would soon be quite engulfed in that swift-flowing sea of mud and melted rock. They stood together silently, overwhelmed by their experiences, as the ship set course for Naples.

The thief who set upon Antonius and that slave who tore the pearls from the monkey's ears were not the only ones to seize their opportunities amid all the confusion. It happened that the Lord Aquila's precious silver goblets had been brought from Rome to grace the wedding-breakfast; and when Tiro and the others fled, Apicius the cook waited last of all, then quickly ran to the chest that held the goblets. It was locked. Desperately he looked round for some implement to force the lock. A bronze statuette stood on a table close at hand. He seized the statue and brought it down upon the chest with all his might. The lock shattered. He opened wide the lid, scrabbling amidst all the plate inside until he found the goblets. He thrust them in a sack and made for the window, levering his bulk into the street outside. The ashes now lay knee-high upon the ground, and he trampled through them as a man may plough his way through fallen leaves or surging surf.

Within the house, Felicia heard the noise of banging as Apicius forced the chest, and the splintering of wood when the lock burst. Then there was silence.

'I am alone,' she muttered feverishly. 'They have all abandoned me.' And she began to whimper like a child.

But she was not alone. When the Lord Aquila had run from the house to seek his wife, he had told Paulina to flee with Tiro. The steward thought she followed him; and later, when he found she was not there, he imagined she was lost amongst the crowd. But Paulina had not left the house. She lingered there irresolutely, lacking the vital urge to save herself by flight. She was indifferent to her fate. In truth, had she not already died with Rufius in the Amphitheatre?

She heard Felicia's frightened whimpering, and went to her. The old slave stared at the girl unbelievingly.

'My lady, you must go!' she gasped. 'Save yourself while you can! Soon—soon it will be too late!'

As she spoke, there came a crashing from the upper storey of the house; the roof had fallen beneath the weight of fiery lapilli. Spreading flames licked at the timbers and scorched the

DOG FOUND AT POMPEII

The body of the dog had decomposed and liquid plaster was poured into the space left in the lava. When the plaster set, the rock surrounding it was chipped away and the plaster cast was obtained.

stonework of the walls. In a little while the ceiling would come down upon their heads.

'It is too late already,' Paulina told her calmly. 'Outside the ashes lie waist-high. Escape is now impossible.'

Felicia looked at her in horror. She had never understood this girl. She was so hard; she seemed to lack all natural human feelings. It was almost as though a marble statue moved and uttered words.

And now the deadly mephitic vapours that arose from the falling ashes began to seep into the house. Felicia and Paulina laboured to draw breath; tears streamed from their smarting eyes.

'It will soon be over,' Paulina whispered painfully. 'Take courage, Felicia!'

Her companion moaned and twisted on the mattress. 'They—say—the gods will grant a man's last prayer,' she gasped. 'Oh my lady, let us pray together!'

Paulina's mouth stretched in the travesty of a smile. She found Felicia's dying piety pathetic. How could a slave hope for immortality?

'There is but one prayer in my heart,' she told Felicia. 'I pray that I may soon be with Lord Rufius in the Underworld!'

The room was like a furnace. They were suffocating. In a moment it would all be over.

Felicia's last conscious thought was not for her son Optatus, nor for Phoebe and her expected grandchild. It was for her favourite nursling, Antonia, the golden child who had become a Vestal. 'Almighty gods, I pray, I pray . . .' But she could not find breath to croak her prayer aloud.

What of the others who fled before the pursuing flood of death? Tiro the faithful steward perished as he rushed along the Stabian road. Iris was fortunate; she met a tavern-keeper escaping on a mule, who took her up beside him. They journeyed as far as Capua together, and she lived with him for the remainder of her life, passing herself off as a freed-woman. Apicius, too, made his escape. He sold the silver goblets he had stolen and at last realized his lifelong ambition to own a cook-stall. Perhaps it was divine retribution that the covetous woman whom he took as his wife put poison into one of his

Suggested Activities

own pies, and thus gained for herself his ill-gotten wealth. Valerius Corvinus died within his villa. He sought refuge in a sealed room, but the choking fumes crept through the fissures of the walls and overcame him. At the last he held a scroll of poetry in his hand. In the Calpurnian house near the Porta Vesuvii, the long-tongued flames had long since licked up the wedding-gown and veil that were intended for his bride.

There were many, many others: a priest who lay beneath the embroidered folds of a costly robe that was become his shroud; a slave who fell clutching a pair of alum-coloured pearls within his fist ... the devout and impious, the worldly and the innocent. For all these that summer day had marked indeed the ending of the world.

Vesuvius was covered by 20 feet of ash. Herculaneum, closer still, was covered by 60 feet of lava which set hard as rock. The inhabitants came back as soon as it was safe and tried to recover their valuables, but were unable to penetrate the ash and rock. Centuries passed and only a legend remained of cities buried under the ground. Then at the start of the eighteenth century a peasant digging to make his well deeper struck on marble. As a result of this excavations of the cities were started. They are still continuing after 200 years, and archaeologists here and elsewhere still find abundant proof of the glory of Greece and Rome.

Suggested Activities

Writing

1. Continue the story of Paul and Julia when they went horse riding the following day.

2. Write about a busy day in the life of a Roman. He might go to the baths (see p. 118), the amphitheatre (see pp. 104–110), the hippodrome (see pp. 119–122) and a dinner (see pp. 117–118).

3. You were at Pompeii when Vesuvius erupted. Write a letter or a diary telling how you escaped.

4. Produce a newspaper at Rome coming out the day after

Pompeii was destroyed. You could include the latest sports news (chariot racing and gladiatorial fights) but Pompeii would take the headlines.

Drawing

1. Draw a picture of a Roman villa or a dining room scene in a Roman house (see pp. 114–115).

2. Draw a chariot race or chariot crash in the hippodrome (see p. 121).

4. Design and draw some murals or mosaics like those found at Pompeii, which could have decorated the walls or floor of a Roman house.

5. Draw a map of the Roman empire at the time of Hadrian (see p. 84).

Acting

1. Act a dining room scene in Roman style.

2. Make some of the scenes on pp. 132–138 into a play and act it.

Finding Out

1. Find out about some of the splendid public buildings which the Romans built at Rome. See Colosseum, temples, baths, forums (market places), basilicas (law courts) and triumphal arches (like the Marble Arch in London).

2. What other volcanoes have erupted? Did Vesuvius inflict the worst damage?

3. Find out about some of the remarkable discoveries which have been made at Herculaneum or Pompeii.

4. Find out how the Roman Empire came to an end (see 'Goths' and 'Huns').

Further Reading

H. and R. Leacroft, *The Buildings of Ancient Rome*.
H. E. L. Mellersh, *Imperial Rome*, Young Historian series.
N. Sherwin-White, *Ancient Rome*, Then and There series.
Geoffrey Trease, *A Ship to Rome*; *Word to Caesar*.
Barbara Ker Wilson, *Beloved of the Gods*.